Ninja Foodi
XL Pro Air Oven
COOKBOOK FOR BEGINNERS

Simple & Delicious Ninja Foodi XL Pro Air Fryer Oven Recipes Combined
with Diverse Cooking Methods Allow You to Enjoy Life to the Fullest

Tracey Crofoot

Table of Contents

Introduction

The Ninja DT250 10-in-1 Air Fryer Oven or the Ninja Foodi XL Pro Air Oven are both from the company's Foodi line. This item is just a countertop convection oven with a variety of uses, if that makes sense.

It offers settings for whole roasting, air frying, air roasting, baking, broiling, toasting settings for bagels and bread, dehydrating, reheating, and producing your preferred pizza. Soon, we'll talk about all those wonderful abilities.

The Ninja DT250 appeals to me because of its sizable capacity. It has the capacity to roast an entire chicken, a 12-lb turkey, or a sizable amount of beef. It can function on par with a full-sized electric oven while using far less electricity.

The Ninja XL Pro Air Oven's quick warmup time is another great feature. In less than 90 seconds, you can begin loading your recipe. That is a lot faster than a conventional convection oven.

You also need to become familiar with its "real surround convection" feature, which is the cherry on top. It does away with the necessity to switch out or rotate your pan.

Two baking pans, recipes, a crumb tray, and two wire racks are included with this Ninja air fryer. So go ahead and use this Ninja Foodi 10-in-1 XL Pro Air Fry Oven - DT250 to experiment with a new recipe.

Fundamentals of Ninja Foodi Smart XL Pro Air Oven

The Ninja Foodi 10-in-1 XL Pro Air Fry Oven DT-250 is carefully made to be user-friendly and to give you a wide range of cooking possibilities.

What is Ninja Foodi Smart XL Pro Air Oven?

You have a lot of cooking options with the Ninja Foodi 10-in-1 XL Pro Air Fry Oven DT250, which is a sizable countertop device. These possibilities include air frying and multiple rack roasting. It provides great toast and functions just like a regular oven.

One of the best-designed toasters we've examined, it features a distinctive and user-friendly digital control panel on the door handle.

To sustain the demands of the entire family, every home needs a nutritious meal. You'll get that from an extremely effective appliance. The extra-large toaster oven and air fry oven with True Surround Convection are known as the Ninja Foodi XL Pro air fryer. Making rapid family meals on two levels is possible with up to 10X the convection power of a conventional full-size convection oven and without the need for rotating. Additionally, it has ten cooking options, including Air Fry, Whole Roast, Air Roast, Bake, Dehydrate, Pizza, Broil, Toast, Bagel, and Reheat. Additionally, it has features like a removable crumb tray, tempered glass door, fits a 12-inch pizza, and digital control and display.

○ For quicker, crispier, and juicier results, use RUE SURROUND CONVECTION, which has up to 10X the convection power of a conventional full-size convection oven.

○ One robust 1800-watt appliance performs 10 VERSATILE FUNCTIONS: Air Fry, Air Roast, Bake, Whole Roast, Broil, Toast, Bagel, Dehydrate, Reheat, and Pizza.

○ COOKING SMART SYSTEM: With the built-in Foodi Smart Thermometer, you can get the ideal doneness, from rare to well done, at the touch of a button and eliminate guesswork.

○ FAMILY QUICK MEALS: Cooking can be completed up to 30% faster than in a conventional full-size convection oven in just 90 seconds.

○ SUPER-LARGE CAPACITY: Fit a 5-lb chicken and a sheet pan of vegetables, two 12-inch pizzas, or a 12-lb turkey on a 2-level flat cooking surface without the need for rotating. For entertaining or weekly meal preparation, prepare two sheet pan dinners at once.

○ AIR FRYER HEALTHY MEALS & CRISPIER RESULTS: Using the Air Fry feature as opposed to conventional deep frying can result in up to 75% less fat (tested against hand-cut, deep-fried French fries). Results can be up to 30% crispier than with a conventional convection oven.

○ DIGITAL DISPLAY HANDLE: Depending on the chosen function, the ideal oven rack placements will be illuminated. To prevent unintentionally altering the cook cycle, display settings freeze while the door is open.

○ COUNTERTOP OVEN PERFECT FOR BAKING: Compared to a top countertop oven, baking outcomes can be up to 50% more uniform.

○ AFFORDABLE LARGE-GROUPS MEALS: For entertaining or weekly meal preparation, prepare two sheet pan dinners at once.

○ modern style
○ has a smart thermometer
○ Convection with full surround for best heat dispersion
○ Simple on the wallet
○ An oven's 90-second preheating time is quicker than usual.
○ Cooking time is 30% faster than in regular ovens.
○ Large capacity; can roast a full chicken and a 12-pound turkey; 10-in-1 functions; BPA-free; 1-year warranty. Air fry, whole roast, air roast, bake, dehydrate, pizza, broil.

Step-By-Step Using It

Functions
Whole Roast: For a full meal, simultaneously roast larger proteins like a 5 pounds of chicken and sides. Or prepare a larger protein on its own, such a 12-lb turkey.
Air Roast: For full-sized sheet pan dinners, thicker proteins, and roasted vegetables, get a crispy exterior and perfectly cooked interior.
Air Fry Foods that would often be fried, such chicken wings, French fries, and chicken nuggets, are air-fried with little to no additional oil.
Bake: Bake everything evenly, from cakes to your favourite cookies.
Dehydrate: Dehydrate fruits, vegetables, and meats for wholesome snacking.
Broil: Brown the tops of casseroles and evenly broil meats, fish, and vegetables.
Toast: Toast up to nine pieces of bread to the shade of brown you choose.
Bagel: When placed cut-side up on the wire rack, up to 9 bagel halves will toast perfectly.
Pizza: Cook pizzas equally, whether homemade or frozen.
Reheat: Warm up leftovers without overcooking them.

Display in Thermometer Mode
Thermometer: Turns on when the thermometer is plugged in and the PRESET or MANUAL button is pressed to activate thermometer mode.
DONENESS display: When in thermometer mode, displays the various doneness levels. To choose doneness, press the TEMP/SHADE +/- buttons.
TARGET: When using a thermometer to display the target temperature, it illuminates.
CURRENT: When using a thermometer, it illuminates to display the thermometer's current temperature.

Display of the Control Panel and Operating Buttons
(Power) Button: Press to turn the unit on and off.
PREHEAT: When the device is preheating, it flashes.
SLICES: When the Toast or Bagel function is used to specify the number of slices, the indicator " SLICES" illuminates.
Time Display: Cooking time is displayed on the timer. When cooking is taking place, time will begin to run out.
Temperature Display: Shows the cook temperature.

Accessing the Cooking Features

Plug the power wire into an outlet and push the button to turn the device on. After ten minutes of inactivity, the device will automatically shut off.
A preheating mode that the Ninja automatically enters lasts always just one minute and 30 seconds. You must have your food ready before you begin preheating because once the preheating is complete, it automatically begins to countdown the cooking time.

Whole Roast
In contrast to the Ninja SP101, this air fryer oven can accommodate an entire chicken or a 12-lb turkey. It can hold a substantial 12-pound

family supper. You can add vegetables and protein to make it a complete dinner if you'd like. We roasted a whole chicken in 50 minutes using the Whole Roast setting. It turned out to be deliciously moist and tender on the inside and golden brown and crispy on the outside.

1. Press the function +/- buttons until WHOLE ROAST shines brightly to pick the function. The time and temperature will be displayed by default. Select the 2 LEVEL button so that "2 LEVEL" displays on the display when cooking two layers.
2. To choose a cook of time up to 4 hours, use the TIME/SLICES +/- buttons.
3. Use the TEMP/SHADE +/- buttons to choose a temperature between 250 and 450 degrees Fahrenheit.
4. To start preheating, press START/STOP.
5. Place the ingredients either directly on the sheet pan or the roasting pan. Place the roasting tray on the sheet pan on the wire rack on Level 1 as soon as the machine beeps to indicate that it has reached preheating temperature. Shut the oven door.
6. Place the sheet pan on Level 1 and use the air fry basket as the second layer on Level 4 when cooking on two layers.
7. The appliance will beep and "COOK END" will appear on the display when cook time is over.

Air Roast

With the exception of the decreased fan speed, air roast functions similarly to the overall roast option. It is used for roasting little bits of meat or vegetables. The Ninja includes a special mode called Air Roast that's made to roast two things simultaneously on two different racks. Two 1-pound pork tenderloins were cooked on the bottom rack using the roast tray placed on a sheet pan, and two pounds of broccoli were cooked on the top rack using the air fryer basket. The vegetables were gently browned and tender-crisp in just 35 minutes, and the pork was browned as well as juicy and delicious.

1. Press the function +/- buttons until AIR ROAST becomes clearly visible to pick the function. The time and temperature will be displayed by default. Select the 2 LEVEL button so that "2 LEVEL" displays on the display when cooking two layers.
2. To choose a cook time up to 4 hours, press the TIME/SLICES +/- buttons.
3. To choose a temperature between 250°F and 450°F, use the TEMP/SHADE +/- buttons.
4. To start preheating, press START/STOP.
5. Put the ingredients on the baking sheet.
6. Place the roast tray on the sheet pan on the wire rack on Level 1 as soon as the appliance beeps to indicate that it has finished preheating. Shut the oven door. Use the sheet pan as the first layer when cooking on two levels, and the air fry basket as the second layer when cooking on level 3.
7. The appliance will beep and "COOK END" will appear on the display when cook time is over.

Air Fry

The ideal location for single-level air frying would be Rack #3. The air fry basket works perfectly for crisping French fries or other starchy vegetables.
To avoid the grease spilling onto the crumb tray, use the roast tray and sheet pan combination when cooking fatty foods like chicken wings or any other protein.
Racks #2 and #4 are suitable for air frying if you need to use two rack levels.
Use high smoke point oils for air fryings, such as canola, avocado, vegetable, or grapeseed. The Ninja comes with a shallow air frying basket for cooking just one layer of food at a time, similar to all toaster oven air fryers. For air frying chicken wings, handmade French fries, Panko-crusted chicken breasts, and Brussels sprouts, it didn't obtain the best ratings, but it did brown and crisp the majority of the food while keeping it moist and soft. It's important to note that some of the items' interiors were dry.

1. 1Press the to choose the function. press the + and - buttons till AIR FRY. glows brilliantly. the standard time temperatures will be displayed. When preparing two layers, pick the button so that it says "2 LEVEL" displays on the screen.
2. Toggle between the TIME/SLICES +/- buttons. choosing a cook time of up to four hours.
3. Press the TEMP/SHADE +/- buttons after that. choosing a temperature range between 250°F–450°F.
4. To start preheating, press START/STOP.
5. Place the contents in the roast tray with a sheet pan and the air fry basket. Put the basket on the sheet pan if the ingredients are fatty, greasy, or

marinated. For dry ingredients, use an air frying basket.

6. Slide the basket into the rack level(s) indicated on the control panel as soon as the appliance beeps to indicate that it has warmed. If using a sheet pan as well, slide both into the oven at the same time, the pan on the wire rack below the basket in the upper rack. Shut the oven door.

7. The appliance will beep and "COOK END" will appear on the display when cook time is over.

Bake

You can prepare up to two trays of bacon, cookies, or muffins using the bake feature at once. To do this, though, you might need to buy a second wire rack. A 9-inch yellow cake baked by the Ninja came out beautifully risen, with a golden brown top and a rich, sensitive texture. Although they were just faintly browned and took a surprising amount of time to bake (15 minutes), the chocolate chip cookies were nonetheless moist and tasty inside. On Racks #2 and #3, you can bake two trays of cookies, bacon, brownies, or muffins.

1. Press the function +/- buttons until BAKE becomes clearly visible to pick the function. The time and temperature will be displayed by default. Select the 2 LEVEL button so that "2 LEVEL" displays on the display when cooking two layers.

2. To choose a cook time of up to 4 hours, use the TIME/SLICES +/- buttons.

3. Use the TEMP/SHADE +/- buttons to choose a temperature between 180 and 450 degrees Fahrenheit.

4. To start heating, press START/STOP.

5. Arrange the ingredients on the baking sheet, cake pan, air fryer basket, or casserole dish.

6. Place the sheet pan on the wire rack as soon as the appliance beeps to indicate that it has reached preheating. Shut the oven door.

7. You can switch on the light during cooking to monitor the process.

8. The appliance will beep and "COOK END" will show up on the display when cook time is finished.

Dehydrat

Yes, you can use this adaptable kitchen tool to dehydrate your favorite fruits, vegetables, and meats to produce scrumptious jerkies. The process will take a few hours, but the outcome will be well worth the wait. We produced fruit chips out of 12 ounces of cut strawberries by using the Dehydrate setting.

For large amounts of dehydration, racks #2 and #3 can be used, or only rack #3.

1. Press the function +/- buttons until DEHYDRATE shines brightly to pick the function. The time and temperature will be displayed by default. Select the 2 LEVEL button so that "2 LEVEL" displays on the display when dehydrating two layers.

2. To choose a dehydration time between 1 and 24 hours, press the TIME/SLICES +/- buttons.

3. To choose a temperature between 85 and 200 degrees Fahrenheit, press the TEMP/SHADE +/- buttons.

4. Put the air fryer basket in the oven with the items inside. To start cooking, close the oven door and select START/STOP.

5. The appliance will beep and "COOK END" will show up on the display when cook time is finished.

NOTE: Buy more dehydration equipment to dehydrate up to four levels simultaneously.

Broil

This broil function can help you prepare food like a professional chef. We cooked four 4-ounce hamburgers on the Broil option and didn't achieve the kind of browning we'd expect from broiling, but the burgers came out moist. It will perfectly brown the top of your food for a more thrilling and better finish. You must master the skill of broiling if you want to improve as a home cook. This feature can be useful for cooking steak or possibly adding a golden brown finish to your casserole dish to make it a little more interesting. By the way, to perform this action, use rack #3.

1. Press the to choose the feature. function the +/- buttons till BROIL shines clearly. the standard time temperatures will be displayed.

2. Select a cook time of up to 30 minutes by pressing the TIME/SLICES +/- buttons.

3. To choose HI or LO, use the TEMP/SHADE +/- buttons.

4. Arrange the ingredients on the baking sheet. Close the oven door after setting the sheet pan on the wire rack and click START/STOP to begin cooking.

5. The device will beep and "COOK END" will appear on the display when the cook time is finished.

Toast

With this device, you may not only replace your dehydrator but also your toaster with a more accommodating replacement, the Ninja Foodi 10-in-1 oven. Up to nine slices of bread can be toasted at once. The Ninja produced flawless toast on the light, medium, and

dark toast settings, uniformly cooked and the right shade of brown. Nine slices of bread can be simultaneously toasted in the oven, and they brown evenly.

1. Press the function +/- buttons until TOAST brightly glows to pick the function. Slice count and level of darkness will automatically default.
2. To choose the number of bread slices, use the TIME/SLICES +/- buttons. 9 slices can be toasted at once.
3. Select the level of darkness by pressing the TEMP/SHADE +/- buttons.
4. Place the wire rack with the bread pieces on it. To start cooking, close the oven door and select START/STOP.
5. The appliance will beep and "COOK END" will appear on the display when cook time is over.

Bagel

The Toast function and the Bagel function both function identically. To make the perfect toast, simply place the bagel cut-side up. However, the bagels didn't toast evenly or at the shade, you'd anticipate for medium doneness on medium.

1. Press the function +/- buttons until BAGEL starts to glow brightly to select the function. The default slice count and amount of darkness will be shown.
2. To choose the number of slices, press the TIME/SLICES +/- buttons. Up to nine bagel pieces can be toasted at once.
3. To choose the level of darkness, use the TEMP +/- buttons.
4. Put the cut-side-up side of the bagels in the centre of the wire rack. To start cooking, close the oven door and select START/STOP.
5. The appliance will beep and "COOK END" will appear on the display when cook time is over.

Pizza

This convection oven can handle both homemade and frozen pizza, whether they are purchased from a store or produced at home. Because of the greater heat dispersion compared to a conventional oven, your food will be baked evenly.

1. Press the function +/- buttons until PIZZA shines brightly to select the function. The default slice count and amount of darkness will be shown.
2. To choose a cook time of up to 4 hours, use the TIME/SLICES +/- buttons.
3. Use the TEMP +/- buttons to choose a temperature between 180 and 450 degrees Fahrenheit.
4. Place the pizza either directly on the wire rack or on a sheet pan. To start cooking, close the oven door and select START/STOP.
5. The appliance will beep and "COOK END" will show up on the display when cook time is finished.

Reheat

For a brief while, I believed that the Ninja Foodi DT250 would be an excellent substitute for microwaves for warming leftovers. With an air fryer, your pizza, fries, or chicken will stay crispy.

1. Press the function +/- buttons until REHEAT brightly glows to pick the function.
2. To choose a reheat time of up to 4 hours, use the TIME/SLICES +/- buttons.
3. To choose a temperature between 100°F and 450°F, use the TEMP/SHADE +/- buttons. To keep food warm, choose below 180°F.
4. Food should be placed on a sheet pan or in a container suitable for the oven, which should then be placed on a wire rack. To start warming, close the oven door and hit START/STOP.
5. The appliance will beep and "COOK END" will show up on the display when cook time is finished.

Tips for Using Accessories

You'll receive a few sheet pans, two wire racks, an air fryer basket, and a roast tray along with the Ninja Foodi Smart XL Pro Air Oven.

You also possess a smart thermometer that is housed in a magnetic container. Like wired headphones, it functions. At the bottom right corner of the handle, there is a jack.

A crumb tray is also present beneath the heating element. Along with removing food debris, it keeps greases from sinking to the bottom of your oven.

For the Ninja DT250's 10 capabilities, those accessories are adequate. For processing a sizable quantity of fruits and beef jerky, the business also sells a dehydrating kit, a 2-inch casserole plate, and a muffin pan.

Using the Foodi Smart Thermometer

Ahead of First Use
Before inserting the cord into the thermometer jack, make sure it is free of any debris and that there are no knots.

1. Take the thermometer out of the packaging. The thermometer on the right side of the device can then be removed by unwinding the cord from the cord wrap. Secondly, connect the thermometer to the jack.
2. When the plug can no longer be inserted into the jack and you hear it click into place, push down hard.
3. Once the thermometer is connected and the thermometer mode is turned on by pressing the PRESET or MANUAL button, the thermometer icon will turn on in the display. Choose the desired cooking mode (such as Whole Roast) and adjust the cooking temperature as necessary.
4. Press PRESET to establish the internal doneness of your food and use the FUNCTION +/- and TEMP +/- buttons to select the food type you want (Rare through Well).
5. Close the hood after adding the accessory needed for the cook function you've chosen. For the preheating to start, press START/STOP.
6. Place the thermometer horizontally into the thickest section of the protein while the machine is preheating. For more information on where to set the thermometer, see the chart on the following page.
7. When the unit has heated up and beeps, open the door, put food inside with the thermometer inserted, and then cover the thermometer cord with the door.
8. To illustrate progress, the display will show the thermometer's current temperature and target temperature. To view the oven temperature and the amount of time since the cook began, press PRESET or MANUAL.
9. When the goal thermometer temperature is attained, the device will automatically shut off. It will beep and say "COOK END" on the display.
10. Before serving, move the protein to a platter and give it time to rest for five minutes.

Straight from the Store

With measurements of 17 x 20 x 13, the Ninja Foodi XL Pro Air Fry Oven DT250 is big and boxy. The glass door has a black plastic handle that houses all of the electronic controls, and the housing is made of stainless steel. This indicates that the product's size is identical to the size of the oven cavity. Additionally, it places the controls at eye level, making them simple to see and use.

Features of the Item
- True Surround Convection offers consistent 2-level cooking without the need for rotation.
- Compared to a full-size convection oven, there is an increase in convection power of up to 10 times.
- Air fry, bake, roast, broil, toast, and more are among the ten features.
- Quick family meals can be prepared in under 35 minutes.
- Large countertop oven with a 12-lb turkey capacity, 1800 watts of power, and a 90-second preheating time
- Rack positioning is made more certain thanks to digital displays.
- healthful family meals prepared in an air fryer
- Dehydrator function on an oven for wholesome snacks

Cleaning and Caring for Ninja Foodi Smart XL Pro Air Oven

On the handle, which is at eye level and is simple to read and reach, are all the settings and the digital readout. The oven's buttons are extremely touch-responsive, and programming the oven is incredibly simple. The display tells you which oven rack position to use when you choose one of the 10 functions. For monitoring the progress, the Ninja has a light inside the oven.

The glass door becomes quite hot during cooking, reaching temperatures of up to 282°F. However, the control handle is still cool enough to operate when cooking. This oven has a running noise level of 61.3 dBA, which is about the same as an electric toothbrush. This was comparable to the noisiest toaster oven that we evaluated.

All of the components lack a non-stick coating. Although the air fryer basket and racks are dishwasher safe according to the manufacturer, hand washing is advised. The components were all quite simple to manually clean.

Daily Cleaning

After each usage, the appliance needs to be completely cleaned.
1. 1 Before cleaning, unplug the appliance from the outlet and give it time to cool.
2. Remove the crumb tray from the oven and empty it.
3. Usage a soft, moist sponge to remove any food spatter from the internal walls and glass door of the appliance after each use.
4. Use a moist cloth to clean the exterior of the main unit and the control panel. It is possible to use a gentle spray solution or non-abrasive liquid cleaner. Before cleaning, apply the cleaner on the sponge rather than the oven's surface.
5. Before placing food on top of accessories, we advise smearing them with the suggested cooking oil or covering them with parchment paper or aluminium foil. Avoid covering roast tray openings with foil or parchment paper.

Thermometer Cleaning

NEITHER the thermometer nor the holder SHOULD be put in the dishwasher.
1. Before cleaning, unplug the thermometer from the appliance and let it cool down.
2. Hand wash the silicone grip and thermometer tip.
3. Soak the silicone grip and stainless steel tip of the thermometer in warm, soapy water to thoroughly clean it. The cord or jack MUST NOT be submerged in water or any other liquid. NEVER use cleaning agents that are liquids close to the thermometer jack. To avoid harming the jack, we advise using compressed air or a cotton swab.

Massive Cleaning

- Before cleaning, unplug the appliance from the outlet and give it time to cool.
- Take out the crumb tray and all other attachments from the appliance, then wash each one separately. To wash the air fry basket more completely, use a non-abrasive cleaning brush. It is advised to hand wash accessories. The wire racks and air fryer basket can be cleaned in the dishwasher, however over time, wear may occur more quickly.
  DO NOT put a sheet pan, a crumb tray, or a roast tray in the dishwasher.
- The interior and glass door of the oven should be cleaned with a soft cloth and warm, soapy water. Abrasive cleansers, scrubbing brushes, and chemical cleaners SHOULD NOT BE USED as they will harm the oven.
  WARNING: DO NOT submerge the main unit in water or any other liquid or put it in the dishwasher.
- 4 Sheet pans and roasting trays should be soaked in warm, soapy water overnight to remove stubborn grease before being washed with a nonabrasive sponge or brush.
- Dry all components completely before re-entering the oven.

A Pro Tip

Put parchment paper or aluminium foil on your sheet pan or roasting tray to stop grease from setting up. If you must, immerse the tray in water for an entire night to soften the accumulation of food particles.

Frequently Asked Questions & Notes

1. The oven won't turn on; why?
    1. Double-check that the power cord is firmly inserted into the outlet.
    2. Place the power cord in an alternative outlet.
    3. If necessary, reset the circuit breaker.
    4. Click the power switch.

2. Is it possible to use a sheet pan rather than an air fry basket with the air fry function?
The results for crispiness may vary, though.

3. Do the cook times and temperatures for conventional oven recipes need to be changed?
Keep an eye on your meal while it's cooking for the greatest outcomes. check out the cook charts in the
For further information on cook times and temperatures, consult the Inspiration Guide.

4. Can I reset the device to its factory defaults?
Even if you disconnect the oven, it will remember the last setting you used for each function.
Press the Light and 2 LEVEL buttons to return the oven to its preset settings for each function.
pressing two buttons at once for five seconds.

5. Why do the heating elements seem to be on and off repeatedly?
This is typical. The oven is made to have accurate temperature control for every task.
by changing the intensity of the heating components.

6. Why does the oven door have steam coming out of it?
This is typical. High moisture foodstuffs could create steam around the door.

7. Why is water flowing from under the door onto the counter?
This is typical. food products having a high moisture content that condense
(such frozen breads) can drip onto the counter and run down the inside of the door.

8. Why is the apparatus producing smoke?
When cooking in Air or other oily food, make sure you're using the roast tray. options include whole roast, air roast, or fry.
If the issue still exists, try running a Toast cycle on shade 7 without any accessories. This will burn. remove any further grease on the smoking heating components.

9. Despite the fact that I used the thermometer, why is my meal overcooked or undercooked?
For the most accurate reading, it's crucial to place the thermometer lengthwise into the ingredient's thickest area. Make sure to give the meal rest for three to five minutes to finish cooking. Refer to the section on using the Foodi Thermometer for more details on recommended doneness when using the MANUAL function and doneness temperatures when using the PRESET function.

10. If the thermometer grip comes in contact with the oven's heated elements, will it melt?
Make sure none of the oven's heating elements come into contact with the grip.

11. How can I get the sheet pan clean?
Soak the sheet pan in water before washing it if food is stuck in it.
When cooking, line the sheet pan with parchment paper or aluminium foil to make clean-up simpler.

12. Why did the device trip a circuit breaker while it was in use?
Because the device consumes 1800 watts of power, it needs to be plugged into a 15-amp circuit breaker. The unit must also be the only appliance connected into an outlet while it is in operation. Make sure the appliance is the only one plugged into an outlet on a 15-amp breaker to prevent tripping the breaker.

4-Week Meal Plan

Week 1

Day 1:
Breakfast: Chives Cream Muffins
Lunch: Spinach Potato Samosa
Snack: Yam Chips
Dinner: Cornish Game Hens with Thai Cucumber Salad
Dessert: Sweet Chocolate Soufflés

Day 2:
Breakfast: Salmon Egg Scramble
Lunch: Roasted Cauliflower
Snack: Cheese and Parsley Stuffed Mushrooms
Dinner: Italian Sausage with Peppers
Dessert: Bananas Bread Pudding

Day 3:
Breakfast: Egg Mozzarella Swirls
Lunch: Eggplant Panini
Snack: Sweet Chicken Wings
Dinner: Swordfish Steaks
Dessert: Boston Cream Donut

Day 4:
Breakfast: Chard Casserole
Lunch: Roasted Carrots
Snack: Bacon-Wrapped Sausages
Dinner: Chicken Lettuce Wraps
Dessert: Exquisite Puff Pastry Apples

Day 5:
Breakfast: Cheesy Chicken Stuffed Peppers
Lunch: Crusty Chili Tofu
Snack: Spicy Nuts
Dinner: Beef Steak
Dessert: Apple Crumble

Day 6:
Breakfast: Mushrooms Cream Spread
Lunch: Crispy Baby Corn
Snack: Tomato Chips with Cheese
Dinner: Air Fried Calamari
Dessert: Berry Pies

Day 7:
Breakfast: Chicken Cheese Bites
Lunch: Crispy Cauliflower Florets
Snack: Hot Dog Roll
Dinner: Orange Duck
Dessert: Chocolate Almond Cakes

Week 2

Day 1:
Breakfast: Ham Quiche
Lunch: Roasted Tawa Veggies
Snack: Potato Chips
Dinner: Spicy Chicken Drumsticks
Dessert: Carrot Cake with Icing

Day 2:
Breakfast: Tuna Salad
Lunch: Spicy Chipotle Nuts
Snack: Cheese Cauliflower Bites
Dinner: Boneless Ribeye Steaks
Dessert: Cherry Turnovers

Day 3:
Breakfast: Sausages and Veggie Egg Casserole
Lunch: Sweet Potato Bites
Snack: Cheese Apple Pie Rolls
Dinner: Italian Squid with Cheese
Dessert: Banana S'mores

Day 4:
Breakfast: Coconut Eggs Spread
Lunch: Mediterranean Veggie Fry
Snack: Pancetta-Wrapped Shrimp
Dinner: Air Fried Tilapia Fillets
Dessert: Nutella Torte

Day 5:
Breakfast: Almond Coconut Oatmeal
Lunch: Baked Parsley Potatoes
Snack: Golden Beet Chips
Dinner: Lamb Stuffed Pita Pockets
Dessert: Orange Butter Cake

Day 6:
Breakfast: Chicken and Cheese Lasagna
Lunch: Potato Au Gratin
Snack: Parmesan Pork Meatballs
Dinner: Turkey Cheese Burgers
Dessert: Sage Red Currants

Day 7:
Breakfast: Okra Egg Hash
Lunch: Parmesan Potato Balls
Snack: Sweet Potato Fries
Dinner: Lemony Ricotta with Capers
Dessert: Hazelnut Cookies

Week 3

Day 1:
Breakfast: Cheese Egg Cups
Lunch: Buttery Mushrooms with Tomatoes
Snack: Eggplant Fries
Dinner: Ricotta Adobo Chicken
Dessert: Currant Cookies

Day 2:
Breakfast: Coconut Cauliflower Rice Pudding
Lunch: Buttery Sweet Potatoes
Snack: Butter Sriracha Chicken Wings
Dinner: Kielbasa with Pineapple
Dessert: Clove Flaxseed Crackers

Day 3:
Breakfast: Cheesy Mascarpone Pancake
Lunch: Colorful Winter Vegetable Patties
Snack: Spicy Chicken Cheese Balls
Dinner: Bread Crusted Fish
Dessert: Coconut Currant Pudding

Day 4:
Breakfast: Delicious Shakshuka
Lunch: Asian Balsamic Fennel
Snack: Easy Ranch Roasted Chickpeas
Dinner: Tasty Thyme Chicken Breast
Dessert: Dark Chocolate Fudge

Day 5:
Breakfast: Cheesy Asparagus Frittata
Lunch: Buckwheat Bean Patties
Snack: Sweet and Salty Snack
Dinner: Kataifi Shrimp with Lemon Garlic Sauce
Dessert: Banana & Vanilla Puffs

Day 6:
Breakfast: Sweet Potato and Black Bean Burritos
Lunch: Roasted Paprika Asparagus
Snack: Homemade Roasted Mixed Nuts
Dinner: Pepperoni Pizza Pockets
Dessert: Delicious Mini Strawberry Pies

Day 7:
Breakfast: Eggs in a Basket
Lunch: Asparagus with Cheese
Snack: No-Corn Cheesy Hot Dogs
Dinner: Spiced Lamb Chops
Dessert: Chocolate Coconut Brownies

Week 4

Day 1:
Breakfast: Homemade Apple Fritters
Lunch: Herby Italian Peppers
Snack: Tomato and Basil Bruschetta
Dinner: Lemongrass Chicken Breast
Dessert: Healthy Banana Oatmeal Cookies

Day 2:
Breakfast: Granola-Stuffed Apples
Lunch: Cheesy Beans
Snack: Mozzarella Sticks
Dinner: Beef Crunch Wraps
Dessert: Delicious Chocolate Cake

Day 3:
Breakfast: Baked Strawberries and Cream Oatmeal
Lunch: Buttery Garlicky Air fried Potatoes
Snack: Seasoned Sausage Rolls
Dinner: Grilled Barramundi with Tangy Butter Sauce
Dessert: Sweet Butter Fritters

Day 4:
Breakfast: Egg, Bean and Mushroom Burrito
Lunch: Fried Brussels Sprouts with Ham
Snack: Ham 'n' Cheese Pies
Dinner: Ground Turkey with Cabbage
Dessert: Pear & Apple Crisp with Walnuts

Day 5:
Breakfast: Fried Apples with Steel-Cut Oats
Lunch: Cheesy Mushrooms
Snack: Healthy Hot Dog Buns
Dinner: Codfish and Oysters Teriyaki with Veggies
Dessert: Crunchy Shortbread Cookies

Day 6:
Breakfast: Caramelized Banana with Yogurt
Lunch: Mushroom Patties
Snack: Crispy Carrot Chips
Dinner: Sirloin Steak with Sausage Gravy
Dessert: Sweet Breaded Bananas

Day 7:
Breakfast: Italian Sausage Sandwich
Lunch: Mexican Sweet Potatoes
Snack: Crispy Ham 'n' Cheese Ravioli
Dinner: Hoisin Glazed Pork Chops
Dessert: Banana & Coconut Cake

Chapter 1 Breakfast

Egg Mozzarella Swirls

Prep time: 15 minutes. | Cooking time: 12 minutes. | Servings: 6

2 tablespoons almond flour
1 tablespoon coconut flour
½ cup mozzarella cheese, shredded
1 teaspoon truvia

2 tablespoons butter, softened
¼ teaspoon baking powder
1 egg, beaten
Cooking spray

1. In a suitable bowl, mix up almond flour, coconut flour, mozzarella cheese, Truvia, butter, baking powder, and egg. Knead the soft and non-sticky dough. 2. Then Select the Air Fry mode. Set the Ninja Foodi Smart XL Pro temperature to 355 degrees F/ 180 degrees C. Select Level "3" and set the time on your Ninja Foodi Smart XL Pro Air Fryer Oven to 12 minutes. Press Start/Pause to begin preheating. Continue to the next step when it is done preheating. 3. Meanwhile, roll up the cheese dough and cut it into 6 pieces. Make the swirl from every dough piece. 4. Grease its air fryer basket with cooking oil spray 5. Place the cheese swirls in the air fryer in one layer, insert its air fryer basket in the level 3 and cook them for 12 minutes until they are light brown. 6. Repeat the same step with remaining uncooked dough. It is recommended to serve the cheese Danish warm.
Per Serving: Calories 199; Fat 17.9g; Sodium 525mg; Carbs 1.1g; Fiber 0.3g; Sugar 0.6g; Protein 9.9g

Sausages and Veggie Egg Casserole

Prep time: 10 minutes. | Cooking time: 20 minutes. | Servings: 4

3 spring onions, chopped
1 green bell pepper, sliced
¼ teaspoon salt
¼ teaspoon ground turmeric

¼ teaspoon ground paprika
10 ounces Italian sausages
1 teaspoon olive oil
4 eggs

1. Select the Air Fry mode. Set the Ninja Foodi Smart XL Pro temperature to 360 degrees F/ 180 degrees C. Select Level "3" and set the time on your Ninja Foodi Smart XL Pro Air Fryer Oven to 20 minutes. Press Start/Pause to begin preheating. Continue to the next step when it is done preheating. 2. Then pour olive oil in its air fryer basket. Add bell pepper and spring onions. 3. Then sprinkle the vegetables with ground turmeric and salt. Insert its air fryer basket into the level 3 of the oven and close the door. Cook them for 5 minutes. 4. When the time is finished, shake its air fryer basket gently. 5. Chop the sausages roughly and add in its air fryer basket. Cook the ingredients for 10 minutes. 6. Then crack the eggs over the sausages and cook the casserole for 10 minutes more.
Per Serving: Calories 281; Fat 15.5 g; Sodium 262 mg; Carbs 27.5g; Fiber 2.2g; Sugar 5g; Protein 8.5g

Chives Cream Muffins

Prep time: 15 minutes. | Cooking time: 12 minutes. | Servings: 4

4 slices of ham
¼ teaspoon baking powder
4 tablespoons coconut flour
4 teaspoons heavy cream

1 egg, beaten
1 teaspoon chives, chopped
1 teaspoon olive oil
½ teaspoon white pepper

1. Select the Air Fry mode. Set the Ninja Foodi Smart XL Pro temperature to 365 degrees F/ 185 degrees C. Select Level "3" and set the time on your Ninja Foodi Smart XL Pro Air Fryer Oven to 12 minutes. Press Start/Pause to begin preheating. Continue to the next step when it is done preheating. 2. Meanwhile, mix up baking powder, coconut flour, heavy cream, egg, chives, and white pepper. Stir the ingredients until getting a smooth mixture. 3. Finely chop the ham and add it in the muffin liquid. Brush the air fryer muffin molds with olive oil. Then pour the muffin batter in the molds. 4. Place this rack in its air fryer basket and place the molds on it. Cook the muffins for 12 minutes (365 degrees F/ 185 degrees C). Cool the muffins to the room temperature and remove them from the molds.
Per Serving: Calories 202; Fat 15.9g; Sodium 720 mg; Carbs 3.9g; Fiber 1.3g; Sugar 1.6g; Protein 12.4g

Salmon Egg Scramble

Prep time: 5 minutes. | Cooking time: 20 minutes. | Servings: 4

A drizzle of olive oil
1 spring onion, chopped
1 cup smoked salmon, skinless, boneless and flaked
4 eggs, whisked

A pinch of black pepper and salt
¼ cup baby spinach
4 tablespoons parmesan, grated

1. In a suitable bowl, mix the eggs with the rest of the recipe ingredients except the oil and whisk well. 2. Select the Air Fry mode. Set the Ninja Foodi Smart XL Pro temperature to 365 degrees F/ 185 degrees C. Select Level "3" and set the time on your Ninja Foodi Smart XL Pro Air Fryer Oven to 20 minutes. Press Start/Pause to begin preheating. Continue to the next step when it is done preheating. 3. Pour the eggs and salmon mix into a pan and transfer to the level 3 of the fryer and cook for 20 minutes. Divide between plates and serve for breakfast.

Per Serving: Calories 315; Fat 28.6 g; Sodium 1020 mg; Carbs 3.1g; Fiber 0.6g; Sugar 1.7g; Protein 11.7g

Chard Casserole

Prep time: 5 minutes. | Cooking time: 15 minutes. | Servings: 4

4 eggs, whisked
1 teaspoon olive oil
3 ounces Swiss chard, chopped

1 cup tomatoes, cubed
Black pepper and salt to the taste

1. In a suitable bowl, mix the eggs with the rest of the recipe ingredients except the oil and whisk well. 2. Grease a suitable pan that fits the fryer with the oil, pour the swish chard mix, place this pan on the rack in the level 3 and cook on "Air Fry" Mode, and set its temperature to 360 degrees F/180 degree C for 15 minutes. 3. Divide between plates and serve for breakfast.

Per Serving: Calories 241; Fat 16.8 g; Sodium 225 mg; Carbs 8g; Fiber 0.4g; Sugar 1.1g; Protein 15.4g

Mushrooms Cream Spread

Prep time: 5 minutes. | Cooking time: 20 minutes. | Servings: 4

1 cup white mushrooms
¼ cup mozzarella, shredded
½ cup coconut cream

A pinch of black pepper and salt
Cooking spray

1. Put the mushrooms in your air fryer's basket, grease with cooking spray and Cook on "Air Fry" Mode, select level 3, and set its temperature to 370 degrees F/185 degree C for 20 minutes. 2. Transfer the cooked mushrooms to a blender, then add the remaining recipe ingredients, pulse well, divide into bowls and serve as a spread.

Per Serving: Calories 161; Fat 7.9 g; Sodium 595 mg; Carbs 10.8g; Fiber 1.7g; Sugar 0.5g; Protein 13.2g

Coconut Eggs Spread

Prep time: 5 minutes. | Cooking time: 8 minutes. | Servings: 4

1 tablespoon olive oil
1 and ½ cup coconut cream
8 eggs, whisked

½ cup mint, chopped
Black pepper and salt to the taste

1. In a suitable bowl, mix the cream with salt, pepper, eggs and mint, whisk, pour into the air fryer 2. Greased with the oil, spread, Cook on "Air Fry" Mode, select level 3, and set its temperature to 350 degrees F/185 degree C for 8 minutes, divide between plates and serve.

Per Serving: Calories 451; Fat 8.4 g; Sodium 134 mg; Carbs 59.6g; Fiber 8.2g; Sugar 4.8g; Protein 32.9g

Tuna Salad

Prep time: 5 minutes. | Cooking time: 15 minutes. | Servings: 4

½ pound smoked tuna, flaked
1 cup arugula
2 spring onions, chopped

1 tablespoon olive oil
A pinch of black pepper and salt

1. In a suitable bowl, put all the recipe ingredients except the oil and the arugula and whisk. 2. Select the Air Fry mode. Set the Ninja Foodi Smart XL Pro temperature to 365 degrees F/ 185 degrees C. Select Level "3" and set the time on your Ninja Foodi Smart XL Pro Air Fryer Oven to 15 minutes. Press Start/Pause to begin preheating. Continue to the next step when it is done preheating. 3. Add the tuna mix to its air fryer basket, stir well, insert its air fryer basket in the level 3 and cook for 15 minutes. In a salad bowl, toss the arugula leaves with the tuna mix, toss and serve for breakfast.
Per Serving: Calories 208; Fat 10.5 g; Sodium 1755 mg; Carbs 26.9g; Fiber 4.1g; Sugar 2.5g; Protein 2.9g

Ham Quiche

Prep time: 10 minutes. | Cooking time: 15 minutes. | Servings: 4

4 ounces ham, chopped
1 cup cheddar cheese, shredded
1 tablespoon chives, chopped
½ zucchini, grated
¼ cup heavy cream
1 tablespoon almond flour

½ teaspoon salt
½ teaspoon black pepper
½ teaspoon dried oregano
5 eggs, beaten
1 teaspoon coconut oil, softened

1. In the big bowl mix up ham, cheese, chives, zucchini, heavy cream, almond flour, salt, black pepper, oregano, and eggs. Stir the ingredients with the help of the fork until you get a homogenous mixture. 2. After this, Select the Air Fry mode. Set the Ninja Foodi Smart XL Pro temperature to 365 degrees F/ 185 degrees C. Select Level "3" and set the time on your Ninja Foodi Smart XL Pro Air Fryer Oven to 15 minutes. Press Start/Pause to begin preheating. Continue to the next step when it is done preheating. 3. Then gently grease its air fryer basket with coconut oil. Pour the ham mixture in its air fryer basket. Insert its air fryer basket into the level 3 of the oven and close the door. Cook the quiche for 15 minutes. 4. Then check if the quiche mixture is crusty, cook for extra 5 minutes if needed.
Per Serving: Calories 235; Fat 18.5 g; Sodium 64 mg; Carbs 9.6g; Fiber 4.1g; Sugar 2.4g; Protein 11.9g

Chicken and Cheese Lasagna

Prep time: 10 minutes. | Cooking time: 25 minutes. | Servings: 2

1 egg, beaten
1 tablespoon heavy cream
1 teaspoon cream cheese
2 tablespoons almond flour
¼ teaspoon salt
¼ cup coconut cream

1 teaspoon dried basil
1 teaspoon keto tomato sauce
¼ cup mozzarella, shredded
1 teaspoon butter, melted
½ cup ground chicken

1. **Make the lasagna batter:** in the bowl mix up egg, heavy cream, cream cheese, and almond flour. Add coconut cream. Stir the liquid until smooth. 2. Then Select the Air Fry mode. Set the Ninja Foodi Smart XL Pro temperature to 355 degrees F/ 180 degrees C. Select Level "3" and set the time on your Ninja Foodi Smart XL Pro Air Fryer Oven to 25 minutes. Press Start/Pause to begin preheating. Continue to the next step when it is done preheating. 3. Brush its air fryer basket with butter. Pour ½ part of lasagna batter in its air fryer basket and flatten it in one layer. 4. Then in the separated bowl mix up tomato sauce, basil, salt, and ground chicken. Put the chicken mixture over the prepared batter in the air fryer. Add beaten egg. 5. Then top it with remaining lasagna batter and sprinkle with shredded mozzarella. Insert its air fryer basket into the level 3 of the oven and close the door. Cook the lasagna for 25 minutes.
Per Serving: Calories 281; Fat 15.5 g; Sodium 262 mg; Carbs 27.5g; Fiber 2.2g; Sugar 5g; Protein 8.5g

Cheesy Chicken Stuffed Peppers

Prep time: 15 minutes. | Cooking time: 5 minutes. | Servings: 2

2 medium green peppers
1 chili pepper, chopped
4 ounces chicken, shredded

1 tablespoon cream cheese
½ cup mozzarella, shredded
¼ teaspoon chili powder

1. Remove the seeds from the bell peppers. 2. After this, Select the Air Fry mode. Set the Ninja Foodi Smart XL Pro temperature to 375 degrees F/ 190 degrees C. Select Level "3" and set the time on your Ninja Foodi Smart XL Pro Air Fryer Oven to 5 minutes. Press Start/Pause to begin preheating. Continue to the next step when it is done preheating. 3. Meanwhile, in the bowl mix up chili pepper, shredded chicken, cream cheese, and shredded mozzarella. Add chili powder and stir the prepared mixture until homogenous. 4. After this, fill the bell peppers with chicken mixture and wrap in the foil. Put the peppers in the preheated air fryer and cook for 5 minutes.

Per Serving: Calories 396; Fat 25.8 g; Sodium 565 mg; Carbs 5.6g; Fiber 0.3g; Sugar 1.7g; Protein 36.4g

Chicken Cheese Bites

Prep time: 15 minutes. | Cooking time: 8 minutes. | Servings: 4

1 cup ground chicken, cooked
½ cup cheddar cheese, shredded
1 egg, beaten

½ teaspoon salt
Cooking spray

1. Put ground chicken and cheddar cheese in the bowl. Add egg and salt and mix up the ingredients until you get a homogenous mixture. 2. Select the Air Fry mode, set the temperature to 390 degrees F/ 200 degrees C. Select Level "3" and set the time on your Ninja Foodi Smart XL Pro Air Fryer Oven to 8 minutes. Press Start/Pause to begin preheating. Continue to the next step when it is done preheating. Spray its air fryer basket with the cooking spray from inside. 3. Then make the small bites with the help of the scooper and place them in its air fryer basket. Insert its air fryer basket into the level 3 of the oven and close the door. Cook the chicken and cheese bites for 4 minutes and then flip them on another side. Cook the bites for 4 minutes more.

Per Serving: Calories 179; Fat 7.5 g; Sodium 242 mg; Carbs 16g; Fiber 0.6g; Sugar 6.8g; Protein 10.6g

Cheesy Asparagus Frittata

Prep time: 15 minutes| Cook time: 15 minutes| Serves: 2-4

1 cup (134 g) asparagus spears, cut into 1-inch (2.5 cm) pieces
1 teaspoon vegetable oil
6 eggs
1 tablespoon (15 ml) milk

2 ounces (55 g) goat cheese
1 tablespoon (3 g) minced chives
Kosher salt and pepper

1. Select the "AIR FRY" function of Ninja Foodi Smart XL Pro Air Oven and select Level 3. Set the temperature to 400°F and time to 5 minutes. Select START/STOP to begin preheating. Toss the asparagus pieces with the vegetable oil in a small bowl. Place the asparagus in a 7-inch (18 cm) round air fryer sheet pan. Place the pan on a wire rack on Level 3. Close the door to begin cooking. Cook it for 5 minutes until the asparagus is softened and slightly wrinkled. Remove the pan. 2. Whisk the eggs with milk and pour the mixture over the asparagus in the sheet pan. Crumble cheese over the eggs and add the chives, if using. Spice with a pinch of salt and pepper. Air fry at 320°F (160°C) for 20 minutes until the eggs are cooked through. Serve immediately.

Per Serving: Calories 173; Fat 13.6g; Sodium 281mg; Carbs 3g; Fiber 1g; Sugar 1g; Protein 10g

Almond Coconut Oatmeal

Prep time: 5 minutes. | Cooking time: 15 minutes. | Servings: 4

2 cups almond milk
1 cup coconut, shredded

2 teaspoons stevia
2 teaspoons vanilla extract

1. In a suitable pan that fits your air fryer, mix all the recipe ingredients, stir well, introduce the pan in the machine and Cook on "Air Fry" Mode, select level 3, and set its temperature to 360 degrees F/ 180 degrees C for 15 minutes. 2. Divide into bowls and serve for breakfast.

Per Serving: Calories 117; Fat 5.8 g; Sodium 1460 mg; Carbs 9.9g; Fiber 3.3g; Sugar 3.3g; Protein 6.7g

Cheese Egg Cups

Prep time: 10 minutes. | Cooking time: 6 minutes. | Servings: 2

2 eggs
2 ounces mozzarella, grated
1 ounces parmesan, grated

1 teaspoon coconut oil, melted
¼ teaspoon chili powder

1. Crack the eggs and separate egg yolks and egg whites. Then whisk the egg whites till the soft peaks. Separately whisk the egg yolks until smooth and add chili powder. 2. Then carefully add egg whites, parmesan, and mozzarella. Stir the ingredients. 3. Brush the silicone egg molds with coconut oil. Then put the cheese-egg mixture in the molds with the help of the spoon. Transfer the molds in its air fryer basket. Insert its air fryer basket into the level 3 of the oven and close the door. Cook on "Air Fry" Mode, select level 3, and set its temperature to 385 degrees F/ 195 degrees C for 6 minutes.

Per Serving: Calories 216; Fat 6.9 g; Sodium 31 mg; Carbs 38.5g; Fiber 5.6g; Sugar 6.7g; Protein 6.7g

Delicious Shakshuka

Prep time: 10 minutes| Cook time: 35 minutes| Serves: 2

Tomato Sauce:
3 tablespoons (45 ml) extra-virgin olive oil
1 small yellow onion, diced
1 jalapeño pepper, seeded and minced
1 red bell pepper, diced
2 cloves garlic, minced
1 teaspoon cumin
Shakshuka:
4 eggs
1 tablespoon (15 ml) heavy cream

1 teaspoon sweet paprika
Pinch cayenne pepper
1 tablespoon (16 g) tomato paste
1 can (28 ounces, or 800 g) whole plum tomatoes with juice
2 teaspoons granulated sugar

1 tablespoon (1 g) chopped cilantro
Kosher salt and pepper to taste

1. Select the "AIR FRY" function of Ninja Foodi Smart XL Pro Air Oven and select Level 3. Set the temperature to 300°F and time to 12 minutes. Select START/STOP to begin preheating. Saute the onion and peppers in hot oil over medium heat, spice with salt, and sauté until softened, about 10 minutes. Add the garlic and spices and sauté a few additional minutes until fragrant. Add the tomato paste and stir to combine. Add the plum tomatoes along with their juice—breaking up the tomatoes with a spoon—and the sugar. Boil the mix to high heat. Lower down and manage to simmer until the tomatoes thicken, about 10 minutes. Turn off the heat. 2. Crack the eggs into a 7-inch (18 cm) round cake pan. Remove a cup of tomato sauce from the skillet and spoon it over the egg whites only, leaving the yolks exposed. Drizzle the cream over the yolks. 3. Place the pan on a wire rack on Level 3. Close the door to begin cooking. Cook for 12 minutes until the whites of eggs are cooked and the yolks are still runny. Remove the pan from the air fryer and garnish with chopped cilantro. Season with salt and pepper. 4. Serve immediately with crusty bread to mop up the sauce.

Per Serving: Calories 429; Fat 32.4g; Sodium 325mg; Carbs 5g; Fiber 1g; Sugar 3g; Protein 28g

Eggs in a Basket

Prep time: 10 minutes| Cook time: 10 minutes| Serves: 1

1 thick slice country, sourdough, or Italian bread
2 tablespoons (28 g) unsalted butter, melted

1 egg
Kosher salt and pepper to taste

1. Install the wire rack on Level 3. Select the "BAKE" function of Ninja Foodi Smart XL Pro Air Oven, set temperature to 300°F and time to 8 minutes. Select START/STOP to begin preheating. Brush the bottom of the air fryer sheet pan with melted butter. Using a biscuit cutter, cut a hole out of the middle of the bread and set it aside. 2. Place bread in the air fryer cake pan. Crack the egg in the bread hole, not breaking the yolk. Season with salt and pepper. Place the cut-out bread hole next to the slice of bread. Place the sheet pan into the air fryer. 3. Bake at 300°F (150°C) for 6 to 8 minutes until the white of egg sets and the yolk is still runny. Using a silicone spatula, remove the bread slice to a plate. Serve with the cut-out bread circle on the side or place it on the egg.
Per Serving: Calories 134; Fat 9.8g; Sodium 394mg; Carbs 2g; Fiber 0g; Sugar 1g; Protein 9g

Streusel French Toast with Aromatic Cinnamon

Prep time: 10 minutes| Cook time: 15 minutes| Serves: 4

Streusel
½ cup (63 g) all-purpose flour
¼ cup (50 g) granulated sugar
¼ cup (38 g) light brown sugar
French Toast
2 eggs
¼ cup (60 ml) milk
1 teaspoon vanilla extract
½ teaspoon cinnamon

½ teaspoon cinnamon
Pinch kosher salt
4 tablespoons (55 g) unsalted butter, melted

Pinch nutmeg
4 slices brioche, challah, or white bread, preferably slightly stale
Maple syrup for serving

1. To make the streusel, combine the flour, sugars, cinnamon, and salt in a medium bowl. Pour the melted butter over the dry ingredients and stir with a fork to combine. Transfer the mixture to a plastic bag and place it in the freezer while you prepare the French toast. 2. To make the French toast, mix the eggs, milk, vanilla, cinnamon, and nutmeg in a medium bowl. Select the "AIR FRY" function of Ninja Foodi Smart XL Pro Air Oven, set temperature to 375°F and time to 5 minutes. Select START/STOP to begin preheating. Line the air fryer basket with parchment paper to prevent sticking. Dunk each slice of bread in the egg mixture, making sure both sides are coated. Hold the bread over the bowl for a moment to allow any excess liquid to slide off. 3. Place the bread in the air fryer basket. Select Level 3. Cook for 5 minutes. Open the air fryer and turn the bread over. Top each slice of bread with 2 tablespoons (40 g) of streusel. Cook for an additional 4 minutes until the bread is crispy and browned and the streusel is puffy and golden. Serve warm with maple syrup.
Per Serving: Calories 227; Fat 9.8g; Sodium 525mg; Carbs 7g; Fiber 2g; Sugar 4g; Protein 28g

Egg, Bean and Mushroom Burrito

Prep time: 10 minutes| Cook time: 15 minutes| Serves: 2

2 tablespoons canned black beans, rinsed and drained
1/4 cup baby portobello mushrooms, sliced
1 teaspoon olive oil
Pinch of kosher salt

1 large egg
1 slice low-fat cheddar cheese
1 eight-inch whole grain flour tortilla
Hot sauce

1. Select Level 3. Select the "AIR FRY" function of Ninja Foodi Smart XL Pro Air Oven, set temperature to 360°F and time to 5 minutes. Select START/STOP to begin preheating. 2. Spray the air fryer sheet pan with nonstick cooking spray, then place the black beans and baby portobello mushrooms in the sheet pan, drizzle with the olive oil, and season with the kosher salt.3. Place the sheet pan into the air fryer; cook for 5 minutes, then pause the fryer to crack the egg on top of the beans and mushrooms. Cook for 8 more minutes or until the egg is cooked as desired. 4. Pause the fryer again, top the egg with cheese, and cook for 1 more minute. 5. Remove the pan from the fryer, then use a spatula to place the bean mixture on the whole grain flour tortilla. Fold in the sides and roll from front to back. Serve warm with the hot sauce on the side.
Per Serving: Calories 277; Fat 12g; Sodium 306mg; Carbs 26g; Fiber 6g; Sugar 2g; Protein 16g

Okra Egg Hash

Prep time: 5 minutes. | Cooking time: 20 minutes. | Servings: 4

2 cups okra
1 tablespoon butter, melted

4 eggs, whisked
A pinch of black pepper and salt

1. Grease a suitable pan that fits the air fryer with the butter. 2. In a suitable bowl, mix the okra with eggs, black pepper and salt, whisk and pour into the pan. 3. Introduce the pan in its air fryer basket. Insert its air fryer basket into the level 3 of the oven and close the door. Cook on "Air Fry" Mode, select level 3, and set its temperature to 350 degrees F/ 175 degrees C for 20 minutes. 4. Divide the mix between plates and serve.

Per Serving: Calories 149; Fat 12 g; Sodium 132 mg; Carbs 10.5g; Fiber 2.6g; Sugar 4.6g; Protein 1.5g

Sweet Potato and Black Bean Burritos

Prep time: 10 minutes| Cook time: 25 minutes| Serves: 6

2 sweet potatoes, cut into a small dice
1 tablespoon (15 ml) vegetable oil
Kosher salt and pepper to taste
6 large flour tortillas
1 can (16 ounces, or 455 g) refried black beans, divided

1½ cups (45 g) baby spinach, lightly packed, divided
6 eggs, scrambled
¾ cup (90 g) grated Cheddar or Monterey Jack cheese, divided
Vegetable oil for heating
Salsa, Roasted Garlic Guacamole, and sour cream

1. Select the "AIR FRY" function of Ninja Foodi Smart XL Pro Air Oven, set temperature to 400°F and time to 10 minutes. Select START/STOP to begin preheating. Toss the sweet potatoes with the vegetable oil, season with salt and pepper, then place in air fryer basket. Select Level 3. Close the door to begin cooking. Cook the potatoes for 10 minutes Remove and set aside. 2. Take a flour tortilla and spread ¼ cup (59.5 g) of the refried beans down the center, leaving a border at each end. Top with ¼ cup (8 g) of the spinach leaves. Sprinkle ¼ cup (27.5 g) plus 2 tablespoons (14 g) of sweet potato cubes on top of the spinach. Top with one-sixth of the scrambled eggs and 2 tablespoons grated cheese. To wrap the burrito, fold the long side over the ingredients, then fold in the short sides and roll. Repeat with the remaining ingredients and tortillas. 3. Wrap each burrito tightly in foil and combine in a large, gallon-size freezer bag. Freeze for up to 3 months. 4. To heat, place the burrito, still wrapped in foil, in the air fryer and cook at 350°F (180°C) for 20 minutes, flipping once halfway through. Remove the burrito from the foil, brush the outside of the tortilla with 1 teaspoon oil, and heat for an additional 3 to 5 minutes, turning once. Serve with salsa, Roasted Garlic Guacamole, or sour cream as desired.

Per Serving: Calories 1052; Fat 50g; Sodium 438mg; Carbs 7g; Fiber 0g; Sugar 7g; Protein 132g

Granola-Stuffed Apples

Prep time: 15 minutes| Cook time: 10 minutes| Serves: 4

4 Granny Smith or other firm apples
1 cup (100 g) granola
2 tablespoons (19 g) light brown sugar

¾ teaspoon cinnamon
2 tablespoons (28 g) unsalted butter, melted
1 cup (240 ml) water or apple juice

1. Install the wire rack on Level 3. Select the "BAKE" function of Ninja Foodi Smart XL Pro Air Oven, set temperature to 350°F and time to 20 minutes. Select START/STOP to begin preheating. Working one apple at a time, cut a circle around the apple stem and scoop out the core, taking care not to cut completely to the bottom. Repeat with the remaining apples. 2. In a small bowl, combine the granola, brown sugar, and cinnamon. Pour the melted butter over the ingredients and stir with a fork. Divide the granola mixture among the apples, packing it tightly into the empty cavity. 3. Place the apples in the sheet pan on the wire rack for the air fryer. Pour the water or juice around the apples. Bake for 20 minutes until the apples are soft all the way through. 4 Serve warm with a dollop of crème fraîche or yogurt, if desired.

Per Serving: Calories 200; Fat 15.6g; Sodium 165mg; Carbs 5g; Fiber 1g; Sugar 2g; Protein 10g

Homemade Apple Fritters

Prep time: 10 minutes| Cook time: 10 minutes| Serves: 5

Fritters
2 firm apples, such as Granny Smith, peeled, cored, and diced
Juice from 1 lemon
½ teaspoon cinnamon
1 cup (125 g) all-purpose flour
1½ teaspoons baking powder
½ teaspoon kosher salt
Glaze
1¼ cups (125 g) powdered sugar, sifted
½ teaspoon vanilla extract

2 tablespoons (26 g) granulated sugar
2 eggs
¼ cup (60 ml) milk
2 tablespoons (28 g) unsalted butter, melted
Vegetable oil for spraying

¼ cup (60 ml) water

1. Select the "AIR FRY" function of Ninja Foodi Smart XL Pro Air Oven, set temperature to 360°F and time to 8 minutes. Select START/STOP to begin preheating. To make the fritters, toss the diced apples with lemon juice and cinnamon in a small bowl, set aside. In a bowl, mix the flour with baking powder, and salt. In a bowl, whisk the sugar and eggs until the mixture is pale yellow. mix in the milk with melted butter. Mix the wet and dry ingredients in the large bowl and stir to combine. Fold in the diced apples. 2. Brush the air fryer basket with oil or line it with parchment paper to prevent sticking. Working in 3 batches and using a spring-loaded cookie scoop, ice cream scoop, or ¼-cup measure, scoop 5 balls of dough directly onto the air fryer basket. Spray the fritters with oil. Place the sheet pan into the air fryer on Level 3. Cook for 7 to 8 minutes until the outside is browned and the inside is fully cooked. 3. Whisk together the powdered sugar, vanilla, and water in a small bowl. Drizzle the glaze over the fritters or dip the tops of the fritters directly in the glaze, letting any excess drip off.
Per Serving: Calories 248; Fat 21.1g; Sodium 429mg; Carbs 2g; Fiber 0g; Sugar 1g; Protein 12g

Cheesy Mascarpone Pancake

Prep time: 10 minutes. | Cooking time: 8 minutes. | Servings: 2

5 eggs, beaten
¼ cup almond flour
½ teaspoon baking powder
1 teaspoon apple cider vinegar

¼ cup cheddar cheese, shredded
1 teaspoon butter
1 tablespoon mascarpone
½ teaspoon sesame oil

1. Brush its air fryer basket with sesame oil. Then in the mixing bowl mix up all remaining ingredients. Stir the liquid until homogenous. Pour it in the air fryer pan and place it in the air fryer. 2. Insert its air fryer basket into the level 3 of the oven and close the door. Select Air Fry mode, cook the pancake for 8 minutes at 360 degrees F/ 180 degrees C Select Level "3". 3. Remove the cooked pancake from the air fryer pan and cut it into servings.
Per Serving: Calories 164; Fat 16.9 g; Sodium 99 mg; Carbs 3.2g; Fiber 0.8g; Sugar 0.2g; Protein 2.3g

Cheese Bacon & Egg Sandwiches

Prep time: 3 minutes| Cook time: 8 minutes| Serves: 2

2 large eggs
1/4 teaspoon kosher salt, divided
1/4 teaspoon freshly ground black pepper, divided (plus extra for serving)

2 slices Canadian bacon
2 slices American cheese
2 whole grain English muffins, sliced in half

1. Slide basket into rails of Level 3. Select the "AIR FRY" function of Ninja Foodi Smart XL Pro Air Oven, set temperature to 360°F and time to 5 minutes. Select START/STOP to begin preheating. 2. Spray two 3-inch ramekins with nonstick cooking spray, then crack one egg into each ramekin and add half the kosher salt and half the black pepper to each egg. 3. Place the ramekins in the fryer basket and cook for 5 minutes. 4. Pause the fryer and top each partially cooked egg with a slice of Canadian bacon and a slice of American cheese. 5. Cook for 3 more minutes or until the cheese has melted and the egg yolk has just cooked through. 6. Remove the ramekins from the fryer and allow to cool on a wire rack for 2–3 minutes, then flip the eggs, bacon, and cheese out onto English muffins and sprinkle some black pepper on top before serving.
Per Serving: Calories 305; Fat 5g; Sodium 618mg; Carbs 26g; Fiber 3g; Sugar 3g; Protein 22g

Creamy Biscuits

Prep time: 15 minutes| Cook time: 18 minutes| Serves: 7

1 cup (125 g) self-rising flour
½ cup (120 ml) plus 1 tablespoon (15 ml) heavy cream

Vegetable oil for spraying
2 tablespoons (28 g) unsalted butter

1. Slide air fry basket into rails of Level 3. Select the "AIR FRY" function of Ninja Foodi Smart XL Pro Air Oven, set temperature to 325°F and time to 18 minutes. Select START/STOP to begin preheating. Place the flour in a medium bowl and whisk to remove any lumps. Make a well in the center of the flour. Slowly pour in the cream in a steady stream and continue stirring until the dough mostly comes together. With your hands, gather the dough, incorporating any dry flour, and form it into a ball. 2. Place it on a floured surface and pat it into a rectangle that is ½ to ¾ inch (1.3 to 2 cm) thick. Fold in half. Turn and repeat. One more time, pat the dough into a ¾-inch-thick (2 cm) rectangle. Using a 2-inch (5 cm) biscuit cutter, cut out biscuits—close together to minimize waste—taking care not to twist the cutter when pulling it up. You should be able to cut out 5 biscuits. Gather up any scraps and cut out 1 or 2 more biscuits. (These may be misshapen and slightly tougher than the first 5 biscuits, but still delicious.)3. Spray the air fryer basket with vegetable oil to prevent sticking. Place it in the air fryer basket so that they are barely touching. Cook for 15 to 18 minutes until the tops are browned and the insides fully cooked. Remove the biscuits to a plate, brush the tops with melted butter, if using, and serve.
Per Serving: Calories 76; Fat 5.7g; Sodium 63mg; Carbs 1g; Fiber 0g; Sugar 1g; Protein 5g

Baked Strawberries and Cream Oatmeal

Prep time: 10 minutes| Cook time: 15 minutes| Serves: 4

1 cup (170 g) sliced strawberries
1 egg
¾ cup (180 ml) milk
¼ cup (60 ml) heavy cream
1 cup (80 g) rolled oats
2 tablespoons (19 g) brown sugar

½ teaspoon baking powder
½ teaspoon cinnamon
½ teaspoon ginger
Pinch salt
1 tablespoon (14 g) unsalted butter

1. Place the sliced strawberries in the bottom of the cake pan for the air fryer, reserving a few for garnish. In a bowl, whisk the egg along with milk and cream and pour it over the strawberries in the pan. 2. In a small bowl, combine the rolled oats, brown sugar, baking powder, spices, and salt. Combine well the dry and wet ingredients in the cake pan and stir to combine. Allow to rest for 10 minutes. Place the reserved strawberries on top of the oatmeal. 3. Install the wire rack on Level 3. Select the "BAKE" function of Ninja Foodi Smart XL Pro Air Oven, set temperature to 320°F and time to 15 minutes. Select START/STOP to begin preheating. Place the sheet pan in the air fryer and bake at 320°F (160°C) for 15 minutes until the oatmeal is warmed through and puffed. Spoon the oatmeal into bowls.
Per Serving: Calories 509; Fat 40.6g; Sodium 525mg; Carbs 8g; Fiber 2g; Sugar 5g; Protein 28g

Fried Apples with Steel-Cut Oats

Prep time: 10 minutes| Cook time: 40 minutes| Serves: 2

1 cup dry steel-cut oats
4 cups water
Pinch of kosher salt

1 large Gala apple, cored and cut into 10 slices
1/8 teaspoon ground cinnamon
1 tablespoon granulated sugar

1. In a medium saucepan, combine the steel-cut oats, water, and kosher salt. Bring the mixture to a boil, reduce the heat to a simmer, and cook uncovered for 30 minutes or until the oats are tender. Set aside. 2. Slide basket into rails of Level 3. Select the "AIR FRY" function of Ninja Foodi Smart XL Pro Air Oven, set temperature to 390°F and time to 10 minutes. Select START/STOP to begin preheating. 3. Spray the fryer basket with nonstick cooking spray, then place the apple slices in the basket and Place it into the air fryer, cook for 10 minutes. 4. While the apples cook, combine the ground cinnamon and granulated sugar in a small bowl and set aside. 5. Remove the apple slices from the fryer and place on a serving plate. Sprinkle 1 teaspoon of the cinnamon sugar mix on the apples. 6. Allow the apples to cool for 5 minutes, then serve on top of the cooked oats.
Per Serving: Calories 183; Fat 3g; Sodium 36mg; Carbs 36g; Fiber 5g; Sugar 8g; Protein 5g

Sweet Pumpkin Oatmeal

Prep time: 10 minutes| Cook time: 10 minutes| Serves: 2

1 cup rolled oats
2 tablespoons raisins
1/4 teaspoon ground cinnamon
Pinch of kosher salt

1/4 cup canned pumpkin puree
2 tablespoons maple syrup
1 cup low-fat milk

1. Install the wire rack on Level 3. Select the "BAKE" function of Ninja Foodi Smart XL Pro Air Oven, set temperature to 300°F and time to 10 minutes. Select START/STOP to begin preheating. 2. In a medium bowl, combine the rolled oats, raisins, ground cinnamon, and kosher salt, then stir in the pumpkin puree, maple syrup, and low-fat milk. 3. Spray the air fryer sheet pan with nonstick cooking spray, then pour the oatmeal mixture into the pan. Place the sheet pan into the air fryer and cook for 10 minutes. 4. Remove the oatmeal from the fryer and allow to cool in the pan on a wire rack for 5 minutes before serving.

Per Serving: Calories 301; Fat 4g; Sodium 140mg; Carbs 57g; Fiber 6g; Sugar 26g; Protein 10g

Smoky Potatoes with Chipotle Ketchup

Prep time: 15 minutes| Cook time: 25 minutes| Serves: 4

2 cups (220 g) diced (½ inch [1.3 cm]) waxy red potatoes
2 teaspoons vegetable oil, divided
Kosher salt to taste
½ cup (80 g) chopped yellow onion
1 cup (150 g) chopped red bell pepper

1¾ cups (420 g) ketchup
2 chipotle peppers in adobo
1 tablespoon (15 ml) adobo sauce
½ teaspoon smoked paprika

1. In a bowl, toss the potatoes with 1 teaspoon of oil and season with a pinch of salt. Slide basket into rails of Level 3. Select the "AIR FRY" function of Ninja Foodi Smart XL Pro Air Oven, set temperature to 400°F and time to 10 minutes. Select START/STOP to begin preheating. Place them in the air fryer basket and cook for 10 minutes. In a bowl toss the onion and pepper with the remaining teaspoon of oil and season with salt. 2. After 10 minutes, add the onion and pepper to the air fryer basket and toss to combine. Cook for further 10 -12 minutes until the peppers are softened and charred at the edges and the potatoes are crispy outside and cooked through. 3. While the vegetables are cooking, prepare the chipotle ketchup. Combine the ketchup, 2 chipotle peppers, and 1 tablespoon (15 ml) of the adobo sauce in a blender and purée until smooth. Pour the chipotle ketchup into a serving bowl. 4. Toss cooked vegetables with the smoked paprika. Serve immediately with chipotle ketchup on the side.

Per Serving: Calories 314; Fat 25g; Sodium 138mg; Carbs 2g; Fiber 0g; Sugar 1g; Protein 17g

Blueberry Oat Squares Bites

Prep time: 10 minutes| Cook time: 14 minutes| Serves: 6

1 cup all-purpose flour
1 cup quick-cook oats
1/4 teaspoon baking powder
Pinch of kosher salt
1/4 teaspoon ground cinnamon
1 large egg, beaten

1/4 cup light brown sugar, packed
1/4 cup unsweetened applesauce
1/4 cup canola oil
1/4 cup low-fat milk
1 cup fresh blueberries
1 teaspoon confectioners' sugar

1. Install the wire rack on Level 3. Select the "BAKE" function of Ninja Foodi Smart XL Pro Air Oven, set temperature to 390°F and time to 14 minutes. Select START/STOP to begin preheating. 2. In a large bowl, whisk together the all-purpose flour, quick-cook oats, baking powder, kosher salt, and ground cinnamon. Set aside. 3. In a separate large bowl, combine the egg, light brown sugar, unsweetened applesauce, canola oil, and low-fat milk. 4. Add the egg mixture to the flour mixture, stirring until just combined, then gently fold in the blueberries. 5. Spray the air fryer sheet pan with nonstick cooking spray, then pour the batter into the pan. Place the sheet pan into the air fryer .Cook for 12–14 minutes or until golden brown and a toothpick comes out clean when inserted through the middle. 6. Remove the pan from the fryer and allow to cool on a wire rack for 10 minutes. Dust the confectioners' sugar on top before cutting and serving.

Per Serving: Calories 236; Fat 11g; Sodium 61mg; Carbs 32g; Fiber 2g; Sugar 12g; Protein 4g

Coconut Cauliflower Rice Pudding

Prep time: 5 minutes. | Cooking time: 20 minutes. | Servings: 4

1 cup cauliflower rice
½ cup coconut, shredded

3 cups coconut milk
2 tablespoons stevia

1. In a suitable pan that fits the air fryer, mix all the recipe ingredients and whisk well. 2. Introduce the in your air fryer and Cook on "Air Fry" Mode, select level 3, and set its temperature to 360 degrees F/ 180 degrees C for 20 minutes. 3. Divide into bowls and serve for breakfast.

Per Serving: Calories 134; Fat 11 g; Sodium 14 mg; Carbs 8.7g; Fiber 4.2g; Sugar 4.5g; Protein 2.2 g

Green Feta Frittatas

Prep time: 5 minutes| Cook time: 11 minutes| Serves: 2

1 cup kale, chopped
1 teaspoon olive oil
4 large eggs, beaten

2 tablespoons water
Pinch of kosher salt
3 tablespoons crumbled feta

1. Select Level 3. Select the "AIR FRY" function of Ninja Foodi Smart XL Pro Air Oven, set temperature to 360°F and time to 3 minutes. Select START/STOP to begin preheating. 2. Spray the air fryer sheet pan with nonstick cooking spray, then place the kale in the pan, drizzle with the olive oil, and Place the pan into the air fryer, cook for 3 minutes. 3. While the kale cooks, whisk together the eggs, water, and kosher salt in a large bowl. 4. Pause the fryer to pour the eggs into the pan and sprinkle the feta on top. Reduce the heat to 300°F and cook for 8 more minutes. 5. Remove the frittata from the fryer and allow to cool in the pan on a wire rack for 5 minutes before cutting and serving.

Per Serving: Calories 216; Fat 15g; Sodium 354mg; Carbs 5g; Fiber 1g; Sugar 2g; Protein 16g

Italian Sausage Sandwich

Prep time: 5 minutes| Cook time: 20 minutes| Serves: 3

1 pound sweet Italian sausage
6 white bread slices

2 teaspoons mustard

1. Select the "AIR FRY" function of Ninja Foodi Smart XL Pro Air Oven, set temperature to 370°F and time to 15 minutes. Select START/STOP to begin preheating. 2. Place the sausage in a lightly greased Air fryer basket. Slide basket into rails of Level 3. Air fry the sausage for 15 minutes, tossing the basket halfway through the cooking time. 3. Assemble the sandwiches with the bread, mustard, and sausage, and serve immediately.

Per Serving: Calories 407; Fat 14.5g; Sodium 336mg; Carbs 31.8g; Fiber 6.6g; Sugar 7.6g; Protein 28.8g

Caramelized Banana with Yogurt

Prep time: 5 minutes| Cook time: 5 minutes| Serves: 1

1 banana, cut into 3⁄4-inch slices
6 oz. nonfat plain Greek yogurt

3 tablespoons Toasted Granola with Almonds

1. Select the "AIR FRY" function of Ninja Foodi Smart XL Pro Air Oven, set temperature to 390°F and time to 5 minutes. Select START/STOP to begin preheating. 2. Spray the air fryer basket with nonstick cooking spray, then place the banana slices in the basket and slide basket into rails of Level 3; cook for 5 minutes. 3. Allow to cool in the fryer for 5 minutes, then remove the banana slices from the fryer. 4. Spread the plain Greek yogurt on a serving plate, then place the banana slices on the yogurt and top with the toasted granola before serving.

Per Serving: Calories 249; Fat 1g; Sodium 96mg; Carbs 40g; Fiber 4g; Sugar 23g; Protein 18g

Chapter 2 Vegetables and sides

Roasted Cauliflower

Prep time: 10 minutes. | Cooking time: 20 minutes. | Servings: 2

1 head cauliflower
½ lemon, juiced
½ tablespoon olive oil

1 teaspoon curry powder
Black pepper and salt to taste

1. Wash the cauliflower and remove its leaves and core. Cut it into florets of comparable size. 2. Cook on Air Roast mode, select level 3. Grease your roast tray with oil and preheat it for 2-minutes at 390 degrees F/ 200 degrees C. Mix fresh lemon juice and curry powder, then add the cauliflower florets and stir. Use black pepper and salt as seasoning and stir again. Cook for 20-minutes and serve warm.

Per Serving: Calories 229 ; Fat 1.9 |Sodium 567mg; Carbs 1.9g; Fiber 0.4g; Sugar 0.6g; Protein 11.8g

Eggplant Panini

Prep time: 10 minutes. | Cooking time: 25 minutes. | Servings: 2

1 medium eggplant, cut into ½ inch slices
½ cup mayonnaise
2 tablespoons milk
Black pepper to taste
½ teaspoon garlic powder
½ teaspoon onion powder
1 tablespoon dried parsley
½ teaspoon Italian seasoning
½ cup breadcrumbs

Salt to taste
Fresh basil, chopped for garnishing
¾ cup tomato sauce
2 tablespoons parmesan, grated cheese
2 cups grated mozzarella cheese
2 tablespoons olive oil
4 slices artisan Italian bread
Cooking spray

1. Cover both sides of eggplant with salt. Place them between sheets of paper towels. Set aside for 30-minutes to get rid of excess moisture. 2. In a mixing bowl, mix Italian seasoning, breadcrumbs, parsley, onion powder, garlic powder and season with black pepper and salt. In another small bowl, whisk mayonnaise and milk until smooth.3. Cook on Air Fry mode and select Level "3". Preheat your air fryer to 400 degrees F/200degrees C and set the time to 15 minutes. Remove the excess salt from eggplant slices. Cover both sides of eggplant with mayonnaise mixture. 4. Press the eggplant slices into the breadcrumb mixture. Use cooking spray on both sides of eggplant slices. Air fry slices in batches for 15-minutes, turning over when halfway done. Each bread slice must be greased with olive oil. 5. On a cutting board, place two slices of bread with oiled sides down. 6. Layer mozzarella cheese and grated parmesan cheese. Place eggplant on cheese. 7. Cover with tomato sauce and add remaining mozzarella and parmesan cheeses. 8. Garnish with chopped fresh basil. Put the second slice of bread oiled side up on top. 9. Take preheated panini press and place sandwiches on it. Close the lid and cook for 10-minutes. 10. Slice panini into halves and serve.

Per Serving: Calories 185; Fat 11g; Sodium 355mg; Carbs 21g; Fiber 5.8g; Sugar 3g; Protein 4.7g

Crispy Baby Corn

Prep time: 10 minutes. | Cooking time: 10 minutes. | Servings: 4

1 cup almond flour
1 teaspoon garlic powder
¼ teaspoon chili powder
4 baby corns, boiled

Salt to taste
½ teaspoon carom seeds
Pinch of baking soda

1. In a suitable bowl, then add flour, chili powder, garlic powder, baking soda, carom seed, and salt. Mix well. 2. Pour a little water into the prepared batter to make a nice batter. Dip boiled baby corn into the prepared batter to coat. 3. Cook on Air Fry mode and select Level "3". Preheat your air fryer to 350 degrees F/ 175 degrees C and set the time to 10 minutes. Line its air fryer basket with foil and place the baby corns on foil. Insert its air fryer basket into the level 3 of the oven and close the door. Cook baby corns for 10-minutes.

Per Serving: Calories 284; Fat 7.9g; Sodium 704mg; Carbs 38.1g; Fiber 1.9g; Sugar 1.9g; Protein 14.8g

Roasted Carrots

Prep time: 10 minutes. | Cooking time: 12 minutes. | Servings: 2

1 tablespoon honey
Black pepper and salt to taste

3 cups of baby carrots
1 tablespoon olive oil

1. In a mixing bowl, mix carrots, honey, and olive oil. Season with black pepper and salt. Cook on Air Roast mode, select level 3 and begin preheating. Cook in air fryer at 390 degrees F/ 200 degrees C for 12-minutes.
Per Serving: Calories 163; Fat 11.5g; Sodium 918mg; Carbs 8.3g; Fiber 4.2g; Sugar 0.2g; Protein 7.4g

Crusty Chili Tofu

Prep time: 10 minutes. | Cooking time: 12 minutes. | Servings: 4

¼ cup cornmeal
15-ounces extra firm tofu, drained, cubed
Black pepper and salt to taste

1 teaspoon chili flakes
¾ cup cornstarch
Oil

1. Line its air fryer basket with aluminum foil and brush with oil. 2. Select the Air Fry mode, preheat your air fryer to 370 degrees F/ 185 degrees C. Mix all the recipe ingredients in a suitable bowl. Place in air fryer, insert its air fryer basket into the level 3 of the oven and close the door. And cook for 12-minutes.
Per Serving: Calories 206; Fat 3.4g; Sodium 174mg; Carbs 35g; Fiber 9.4g; Sugar 5.9g; Protein 10.6g

Delicious Fried Corn

Prep time: 10 minutes. | Cooking time: 10 minutes. | Servings: 8

4 ears of corn
Black pepper and salt to taste

3 teaspoons vegetable oil

1. Remove the husks from corn, wash and pat them dry. Cut if needed to fit into air fryer basket. 2. Drizzle with vegetable oil and season with black pepper and salt. Insert its air fryer basket into the level 3 of the oven and close the door. Cook on "Air Fry" Mode, select level 3, and set its temperature to 400 degrees F/200 degrees C for 10-minutes.
Per Serving: Calories 208; Fat 5g; Sodium 1205mg; Carbs 34.1g; Fiber 7.8g; Sugar 2.5g; Protein 5.9g

Crispy Cauliflower Florets

Prep time: 10 minutes. | Cooking time: 20 minutes. | Servings: 2

1 egg, beaten
2 tablespoons parmesan cheese, grated
2 cups cauliflower florets, boiled
¼ cup almond flour
1 tablespoon olive oil

Salt to taste
½ tablespoon mixed herbs
½ teaspoon chili powder
½ teaspoon garlic powder
½ cup breadcrumbs

1. In a suitable bowl, mix garlic powder, breadcrumbs, chili powder, mixed herbs, salt, and cheese. 2. Add olive oil to the breadcrumb mixture and mix well. 3. Place flour in a suitable bowl and place the egg in another bowl. 4. Dip the cauliflower florets into the beaten egg, then in flour, and coat with breadcrumbs. 5. Cook on Air Fry mode and Select Level "3", preheat your air fryer to 350 degrees F/ 175 degrees C and set the time to 10 minutes. Place the coated cauliflower florets inside air fryer basket. Insert its air fryer basket into the level 3 of the oven and close the door. And cook for 20-minutes.
Per Serving: Calories 270; Fat 14.6g; Sodium 394mg; Carbs 31.3g; Fiber 7.5g; Sugar 9.7g; Protein 6.4g

Spinach Potato Samosa

Prep time: 10 minutes. | Cooking time: 15 minutes. | Servings: 2

1 ½ cups of almond flour
½ teaspoon baking soda
1 teaspoon garam masala
1 teaspoon coriander, chopped
¼ cup green peas

½ teaspoon sesame seeds
¼ cup potatoes, boiled, small chunks
2 tablespoons olive oil
¾ cup boiled and blended spinach puree
Salt and chili powder to taste

1. In a suitable bowl, mix baking soda, salt, and flour to make the prepared dough. Add 1 tablespoon of oil. 2. Add the spinach puree and mix until the prepared dough is smooth. Place in fridge for twenty-minutes. 3. In the pan add one tablespoon of oil, then add potatoes, peas and cook for 5-minutes. 4. Add the sesame seeds, garam masala, coriander, and stir. Knead the prepared dough and make the small ball using a rolling pin. 5. Form balls, make into cone shapes, which are then filled with stuffing that is not yet fully cooked. Make sure flour sheets are well sealed. 6. Preheat on "Air Fry" Mode, and set its temperature to 390 degrees F/ 200 degrees C. Place samosa in air fryer basket. Insert its air fryer basket into the level 3 of the oven and close the door. and cook for 15 minutes.

Per Serving: Calories 122; Fat 1.8g; Sodium 794mg; Carbs 17g; Fiber 8.9g; Sugar 1.6g; Protein 1.9g

Roasted Tawa Veggies

Prep time: 10 minutes. | Cooking time: 25 minutes. | Servings: 4

¼ cup okra
2 teaspoons garam masala
1 teaspoon red chili powder
1 teaspoon amchur powder
¼ cup taro root

¼ cup potato
¼ cup eggplant
Salt to taste
Olive oil for brushing

1. Cut potato and taro root into fries and soak in salt water for 10 minutes. Cut okra and eggplant into four pieces. Rinse potatoes and taro root and pat dry. 2. Add the spices to potatoes, taro roots, okra, and eggplant. 3. Cooke on Air Roast mode and select level 3. Brush pan with oil and preheat to 390 degrees F/ 200 degrees C and cook for 10 minutes. Lower the heat to 355 degrees F /180 degrees C and cook for an additional 15-minutes.

Per Serving: Calories 288; Fat 6.9g; Sodium 761mg; Carbs 46g; Fiber 4g; Sugar 12g; Protein 9.6g

Mediterranean Veggie Fry

Prep time: 10 minutes. | Cooking time: 20 minutes. | Servings: 4

1 large zucchini, sliced
1 green pepper, sliced
1 large parsnip, peeled and cubed
Black pepper and salt to taste
2 tablespoons honey
2 cloves garlic, crushed

1 teaspoon mixed herbs
1 teaspoon mustard
6 tablespoons olive oil, divided
4 cherry tomatoes
1 medium carrot, peeled and cubed

1. Add the zucchini, green pepper, parsnip, cherry tomatoes, carrot to bottom of air fryer. Cover ingredients with 3 tablespoons of oil and adjust the time to 15-minutes. Cook on "Air Fry" Mode, select level 3, and set its temperature to 360 degrees F. 2. Prepare your marinade by combining remaining ingredients in air fryer safe baking dish. Mix marinade and vegetables in baking dish and stir well. 3. Sprinkle with black pepper and salt. Cook it at 390 degrees F/ 200 degrees C for 5-minutes.

Per Serving: Calories 260; Fat 16g; Sodium 585mg; Carbs 3.1g; Fiber 1.3g; Sugar 0.2g; Protein 5.5g

Sweet Potato Bites

Prep time: 10 minutes. | Cooking time: 15 minutes. | Servings: 2

2 sweet potatoes, diced
½ cup parsley, chopped
2 tablespoons honey

2 tablespoons olive oil
2 teaspoons cinnamon
1 teaspoon red chili flakes

1. Select the Air Fry mode, preheat your air fryer to 350 degrees F/ 175 degrees C. Add all the recipe ingredients in a suitable mixing bowl and toss well. 2. Place the sweet potato mixture into air fryer basket. Insert its air fryer basket into the level 3 of the oven and close the door. 3. Cook in preheated air fryer for 15-minutes.

Per Serving: Calories 266 ; Fat 6.3g; Sodium 193mg; Carbs 39.1g; Fiber 7.2g; Sugar 5.2g; Protein 14.8g

Spicy Chipotle Nuts

Prep time: 10 minutes. | Cooking time: 4 minutes. | Servings: 8

2 cups mixed nuts
1 teaspoon chipotle chili powder
1 teaspoon salt

1 teaspoon pepper
1 tablespoon butter, melted
1 teaspoon ground cumin

1. In a suitable bowl, put the mixed nuts, then add all the recipe ingredients and toss to coat. Cook on Air Fry mode, preheat your air fryer to 350 degrees F/ 175 degrees C for 4 minutes. 2. Add mixed nuts into air fryer basket, insert its air fryer basket into the level 3 of the oven and close the door. And cook for 4-minutes.

Per Serving: Calories 350; Fat 2.6g; Sodium 358mg; Carbs 64.6g; Fiber 14.4g; Sugar 3.3g; Protein 19.9g

Buttery Sweet Potatoes

Prep time: 15 minutes| Cook time: 25 minutes| Serves: 2

2 sweet potatoes, peeled and halved
1 tablespoon butter, melted

1 teaspoon dried dill weed
Sea salt and red pepper flakes, crushed

1. Install the wire rack on Level 3. Select the "AIR ROAST" function of Ninja Foodi Smart XL Pro Air Oven, set temperature to 380°F and time to 15 minutes. Select START/STOP to begin preheating. Toss the sweet potatoes with the remaining ingredients. 2. Cook the sweet potatoes for 15 minutes, shaking them halfway through the cooking time. 3. Taste and adjust the seasonings. Bon appétit!

Per Serving: Calories 163; Fat 5.8g; Sodium 323mg; Carbs 26.2g; Fiber 3.6g; Sugar 5.4g; Protein 2g

Baked Parsley Potatoes

Prep time: 10 minutes. | Cooking time: 40 minutes. | Servings: 3

3 baking potatoes, washed
Parsley for garnishing
1 tablespoon olive oil

Salt to taste
2 garlic cloves, crushed

1. **Prepare the potatoes:** make holes using a fork in them. Season potatoes with salt and cover with garlic puree and olive oil. 2. Layer the potatoes in its air fryer basket and Insert its air fryer basket into the level 3 of the oven and close the door. Cook on "Air Fry" Mode, select level 3, and set its temperature to 390 degrees F/ 200 degrees C and cook for 40-minutes.

Per Serving: Calories 248 ; Fat 30g; Sodium 660mg; Carbs 5g; Fiber 0g; Sugar 0g; Protein 4g

Potato Au Gratin

Prep time: 10 minutes. | Cooking time: 15 minutes. | Servings: 4

¼ cup milk
3 tablespoons cheddar cheese, grated
3 potatoes, peeled and sliced
¼ teaspoon nutmeg

¼ teaspoon pepper
¼ teaspoon salt
¼ cup coconut cream

1. Select the Air Fry mode, preheat air fryer to 400 degrees F/200 degrees C . 2. Add the cream and milk into a suitable bowl and season with salt, pepper, and nutmeg. Coat potato slices in milk and cream mixture. 3. Spread the potato slices in an oven-safe dish and pour remaining cream on top of potato slices. 4. Sprinkle the top with grated cheese. 5. Place into air fryer basket, insert its air fryer basket into the level 3 of the oven and close the door. And cook for 15-minutes.
Per Serving: Calories 297 ; Fat 1g; Sodium 291mg; Carbs 35g; Fiber 1g; Sugar 9g; Protein 2g

Parmesan Potato balls

Prep time: 10 minutes. | Cooking time: 4 minutes. | Servings: 4

4 potatoes, diced and boiled
2 tablespoons flour
1 egg yolk
1 tablespoon olive oil

3 tablespoons breadcrumbs
Nutmeg to taste
Black pepper and salt to taste
3 tablespoons parmesan cheese

1. Mash potatoes and add all the recipe ingredients except breadcrumbs and oil to the bowl. 2. Mix ingredients and make into medium size balls. Mix breadcrumbs and olive oil separately. Coat balls with breadcrumbs. 3. Preheat on "Air Fry" Mode, and set its temperature to 390 degrees F/ 200 degrees C and cook for 4 minutes.
Per Serving: Calories 257; Fat 10.4g; Sodium 431mg; Carbs 20g; Fiber 0g; Sugar 1.6g; Protein 2g

Roasted Fennel

Prep time: 5 minutes| Cook time: 15 minutes| Serves: 4

1-pound fennel bulbs, trimmed and sliced
2 tablespoons olive oil
1 teaspoon fresh garlic, minced

1 teaspoon dried parsley flakes
Kosher salt and ground black pepper, to taste

1. Select the "AIR FRY" function of Ninja Foodi Smart XL Pro Air Oven, set temperature to 370°F and time to 15 minutes. Select START/STOP to begin preheating. Toss all ingredients in a mixing bowl. 2. Place the basket in the air fryer on Level 3; Cook the fennel for about 15 minutes or until cooked through, check your fennel halfway through the cooking time. Bon appétit!
Per Serving: Calories 97; Fat 6.9g; Sodium 211mg; Carbs 8.4g; Fiber 3.5g; Sugar 4.4g; Protein 1.4g

Colorful Winter Vegetable Patties

Prep time: 5 minutes| Cook time: 15 minutes| Serves: 3

1 carrot, shredded
1 parsnip, shredded
1 onion, chopped
1 garlic clove, minced

½ cup all-purpose flour
1 teaspoon cayenne pepper
Sea salt and ground black pepper, to taste
2 eggs, whisked

1. Select Level 3. Select the "AIR FRY" function of Ninja Foodi Smart XL Pro Air Oven, set temperature to 380°F and time to 15 minutes. Select START/STOP to begin preheating. Mix all of the ingredients until everything is well combined. Form the mixture into three patties. 2. Place the basket with patties into the air fryer; cook the burgers for about 15 minutes or until cooked through. Bon appétit!
Per Serving: Calories 184; Fat 3.3g; Sodium 366mg; Carbs 8g; Fiber 4.3g; Sugar 5.6g; Protein 8g

Buttery Mushrooms with Tomatoes

Prep time: 5 minutes| Cook time: 10 minutes| Serves: 4

1 pound cremini mushrooms, sliced
1 large tomato, sliced
2 tablespoons butter, melted
1 teaspoon rosemary, minced

1 teaspoon parsley, minced
1 teaspoon garlic, minced
Coarse sea salt and ground black pepper, to taste

1. Select Level 3. Select the "AIR FRY" function of Ninja Foodi Smart XL Pro Air Oven, set temperature to 400°F and time to 7 minutes. Select START/STOP to begin preheating. Toss the mushrooms and tomatoes with the remaining ingredients. Toss until they are well coated on all sides. 2. Arrange the mushrooms in the Air Fryer basket. 3. Place the basket into the air fryer, and cook your mushrooms for about 7 minutes, shaking the basket halfway through the cooking time. Bon appétit!
Per Serving: Calories 84; Fat 6.3g; Sodium 132mg; Carbs 6.1g; Fiber 4.1g; Sugar 2g; Protein 2.8g

Asparagus with Cheese

Prep time: 5 minutes| Cook time: 10 minutes| Serves: 4

1-pound asparagus, trimmed
1 tablespoon sesame oil
½ teaspoon onion powder

½ teaspoon granulated garlic
Sea salt and cayenne pepper, to taste
½ cup Pecorino cheese, preferably freshly grated

1. Select the "AIR FRY" function of Ninja Foodi Smart XL Pro Air Oven, set temperature to 400°F and time to 6 minutes. Select START/STOP to begin preheating. Toss the asparagus with the sesame oil, onion powder, granulated garlic, salt, and cayenne pepper. Arrange the asparagus spears in the air fryer basket. 2. Place the basket in the air fryer on Level 3. Cook the asparagus for about 6 minutes, tossing them halfway through the cooking time. 3. Top the asparagus with the cheese. Bon appétit!
Per Serving: Calories 120; Fat 8.5g; Sodium 244mg; Carbs 5.9g; Fiber 2.8g; Sugar 2.6g; Protein 6.9g

Cheesy Beans

Prep time: 5 minutes| Cook time: 9 minutes| Serves: 2

½ pound green beans
1 tablespoon sesame oil

Sea salt and ground black pepper, to taste
2 ounces cheddar cheese, grated

1. Install the wire rack on Level 3. Select the "BAKE" function of Ninja Foodi Smart XL Pro Air Oven, set temperature to 380°F and time to 7 minutes. Select START/STOP to begin preheating. Toss the green beans with the sesame oil; then, arrange them in the air fryer basket. 2. Place the basket in the air fryer, cook the green beans for 7 minutes, tossing the basket halfway through the cooking time. 3.Toss the warm green beans with the salt, black pepper, and cheese; stir to combine well. Enjoy!
Per Serving: Calories 154; Fat 9.6g; Sodium 444mg; Carbs 13g; Fiber 3.4g; Sugar 6.9g; Protein 6.4g

Brussels Sprouts with Cheese

Prep time: 5 minutes| Cook time: 13 minutes| Serves: 4

1 pound Brussels sprouts, trimmed
1 tablespoon olive oil

Sea salt and ground black pepper, to taste
4 ounces Provolone cheese, crumbled

1. Select the "AIR FRY" function of Ninja Foodi Smart XL Pro Air Oven, set temperature to 380°F and time to 10 minutes. Select START/STOP to begin preheating. Toss the Brussels sprouts with the olive oil and spices until they are well coated on all sides; then, arrange the Brussels sprouts in the Air Fryer basket. 2. Slide basket into rails of Level 3, cook the Brussels sprouts for 10 minutes, shaking the basket halfway through the cooking time. 3.Toss the Brussels sprouts with the cheese and serve warm. Enjoy!
Per Serving: Calories 183; Fat 11.8g; Sodium 144mg; Carbs 11.8g; Fiber 4.5g; Sugar 3.2g; Protein 11.4g

Asian Balsamic Fennel

Prep time: 5 minutes| Cook time: 15 minutes| Serves: 4

1-pound fennel bulbs, trimmed and sliced
2 tablespoons sesame oil
Sea salt and ground black pepper, to taste
1 teaspoon red pepper flakes, crushed

1 tablespoon balsamic vinegar
1 tablespoon soy sauce
1 tablespoon sesame seeds, lightly toasted

1. Select Level 3. Select the "AIR FRY" function of Ninja Foodi Smart XL Pro Air Oven, set temperature to 370°F and time to 15 minutes. Select START/STOP to begin preheating. Toss the fennel with the sesame oil, salt, black pepper, and red pepper flakes. 2. Place the fennel in air fryer basket and cook the fennel for about 15 minutes or until cooked through; check your fennel halfway through the cooking time. 3.Toss the warm fennel with vinegar, soy sauce, and sesame seeds. Bon appétit!
Per Serving: Calories 114; Fat 8.3g; Sodium 144mg; Carbs 9.1g; Fiber 3.8g; Sugar 5.2g; Protein 2g

Roasted Paprika Asparagus

Prep time: 5 minutes| Cook time: 10 minutes| Serves: 3

¾-pound fresh asparagus, trimmed
Coarse sea salt and ground black pepper, to taste

1 teaspoon paprika
2 tablespoons olive oil

1. Install the wire rack on Level 3. Select the "AIR ROAST" function of Ninja Foodi Smart XL Pro Air Oven, set temperature to 400°F and time to 6 minutes. Select START/STOP to begin preheating. Toss the asparagus with salt, black pepper, paprika, and olive oil. Transfer the asparagus spears to the air fryer basket. Place the basket in the air fryer. 2.Cook the asparagus for about 6 minutes, tossing them halfway through the cooking time. Bon appétit!
Per Serving: Calories 110; Fat 6.3g; Sodium 304mg; Carbs 9.2g; Fiber 2.9g; Sugar 2.9g; Protein 2.9g

Buckwheat Bean Patties

Prep time: 5 minutes| Cook time: 15 minutes| Serves: 4

1 cup buckwheat, soaked overnight and rinsed
1 cup canned kidney beans, drained and well rinsed
¼ cup walnuts, chopped
1 tablespoon olive oil

1 small onion, chopped
1 teaspoon smoked paprika
Sea salt and ground black pepper, to taste
½ cup bread crumbs

1. Select the "AIR FRY" function of Ninja Foodi Smart XL Pro Air Oven, set temperature to 380°F and time to 15 minutes. Select START/STOP to begin preheating. Mix all ingredients until everything is well combined. Form the mixture into four patties and arrange them in a lightly greased air fryer basket. 2. Slide basket into rails of Level 3 .Cook the burgers for about 15 minutes until cooked through. Turn them over halfway through the cooking time. Bon appétit!
Per Serving: Calories 198; Fat 8.7g; Sodium 236mg; Carbs 24.2g; Fiber 5.3g; Sugar 2.2g; Protein 8g

Fried Brussels Sprouts with Ham

Prep time: 5 minutes| Cook time: 15 minutes| Serves: 4

1 pound Brussels sprouts, trimmed
1 tablespoon peanut oil

Sea salt and freshly ground black pepper, to season
2 (ounces) ham, diced

1. Select the "AIR FRY" function of Ninja Foodi Smart XL Pro Air Oven, set temperature to 380°F and time to 13 minutes. Select START/STOP to begin preheating. Toss the Brussels sprouts with the remaining ingredients; then, arrange the Brussels sprouts in the Air Fryer basket. 2. Slide basket into rails of Level 3; cook the Brussels sprouts for 13 minutes, shaking the basket halfway through the cooking time. 3. Serve warm and enjoy!

Per Serving: Calories 93; Fat 4.3g; Sodium 311mg; Carbs 10.2g; Fiber 4.3g; Sugar 2.4g; Protein 6.2g

Buttery Garlicky Air fried Potatoes

Prep time: 10 minutes| Cook time: 18 minutes| Serves: 3

¾ pound potatoes, quartered
1 tablespoon butter, melted
1 teaspoon garlic, pressed

1 teaspoon dried oregano
Sea salt and ground black pepper, to taste

1. Select the "AIR FRY" function of Ninja Foodi Smart XL Pro Air Oven, set temperature to 400°F and time to 18 minutes. Select START/STOP to begin preheating. Toss the potatoes with the remaining ingredients until well coated on all sides. 2. Arrange the potatoes in the Air Fryer basket. 3. Slide basket into rails of Level 3; cook the potatoes for about 18 minutes, shaking the basket halfway through the cooking time. 4.Serve warm and enjoy!

Per Serving: Calories 123; Fat 4g; Sodium 213mg; Carbs 20.1g; Fiber 2.5g; Sugar 0.9g; Protein 2.3g

Cheesy Mushrooms

Prep time: 5 minutes| Cook time: 10 minutes| Serves: 4

1-pound chestnut mushrooms, quartered
1 tablespoon olive oil
1 garlic clove, pressed

Sea salt and ground black pepper, to taste
4 tablespoons Pecorino Romano cheese, shredded

1. Select the "AIR FRY" function of Ninja Foodi Smart XL Pro Air Oven, set temperature to 400°F and time to 7 minutes. Select START/STOP to begin preheating. Toss the mushrooms with the oil, garlic, salt, and black pepper. Toss until they are well coated on all sides. 2. Arrange the mushrooms in the Air Fryer basket. Slide basket into rails of Level 3. 3.Cook your mushrooms for about 7 minutes, shaking the basket halfway through the cooking time.4.Afterwards, toss the mushrooms with the cheese and serve immediately!

Per Serving: Calories 83; Fat 5.1g; Sodium 136mg; Carbs 6.4g; Fiber 1.7g; Sugar 3.4g; Protein 4g

Mexican Sweet Potatoes

Prep time: 15 minutes| Cook time: 35 minutes| Serves: 4

1 pound sweet potatoes, scrubbed, prick with a fork
1 tablespoon olive oil
Coarse sea salt and ground black pepper, to taste

½ teaspoon cayenne pepper
4 tablespoons salsa

1. Slide basket into rails of Level 3. Select the "AIR FRY" function of Ninja Foodi Smart XL Pro Air Oven, set temperature to 380°F and time to 35 minutes. Select START/STOP to begin preheating. Sprinkle the sweet potatoes with olive oil, salt, black pepper, and cayenne pepper.2. Place the basket in the air fryer, cook the sweet potatoes for 35 minutes, checking them halfway through the cooking time.3.Split the tops open with a knife. Top each potato with salsa and serve. Bon appétit!

Per Serving: Calories 128; Fat 3.5g; Sodium 146mg; Carbs 22.1g; Fiber 3g; Sugar 2.1g; Protein 3g

Herby Italian Peppers

Prep time: 10 minutes| Cook time: 15 minutes| Serves: 3

3 Italian peppers, seeded and halved
1 tablespoon olive oil
Kosher salt and ground black pepper, to taste
1 teaspoon cayenne pepper

1 tablespoon fresh parsley, chopped
1 tablespoon fresh basil, chopped
1 tablespoon fresh chives, chopped

1. Select the "AIR FRY" function of Ninja Foodi Smart XL Pro Air Oven, set temperature to 400°F and time to 5 minutes. Select START/STOP to begin preheating. Toss the peppers with the olive oil, salt, black pepper, and cayenne pepper; place the peppers in the air fryer basket. 2. Place the basket in the air fryer on Level 3. Cook the peppers for about 13 minutes, shaking the basket halfway through the cooking time. 3.Taste, adjust the seasonings, and serve with the fresh herbs. Bon appétit!

Per Serving: Calories 77; Fat 4.6g; Sodium 359mg; Carbs 7.2g; Fiber 2.4g; Sugar 5g; Protein 1.4g

Egg-Stuffed Peppers

Prep time: 5 minutes| Cook time: 15 minutes| Serves: 3

3 bell peppers, seeded and halved
1 tablespoon olive oil
3 eggs

3 tablespoons green onion, chopped
Sea salt and ground black pepper

1. Select Level 3. Select the "AIR FRY" function of Ninja Foodi Smart XL Pro Air Oven, set temperature to 390°F and time to 10 minutes. Select START/STOP to begin preheating. Toss the peppers with the oil; place them in the Air Fryer basket. 2. Crack an egg into each bell pepper half. Sprinkle your peppers with the salt and black pepper. 3. Place the basket in the air fryer, cook the peppers for about 10 minutes. Top the peppers with green onions. Continue to cook for 4 minutes more. Bon appétit!

Per Serving: Calories 143; Fat 9.1g; Sodium 203mg; Carbs 7.8g; Fiber 2.6g; Sugar 5.4g; Protein 6.4g

Spicy Chinese Asparagus

Prep time: 5 minutes| Cook time: 10 minutes| Serves: 4

1-pound asparagus
4 teaspoons Chinese chili oil
½ teaspoon garlic powder

1 tablespoon soy sauce
½ teaspoon red pepper flakes, crushed

1. Select the "AIR FRY" function of Ninja Foodi Smart XL Pro Air Oven, set temperature to 400°F and time to 6 minutes. Select START/STOP to begin preheating. Toss the asparagus with the remaining ingredients. Arrange the asparagus spears in the Air Fryer basket. 2. Slide basket into rails of Level 3, cook the asparagus for about 6 minutes, tossing them halfway through the cooking time. Bon appétit!

Per Serving: Calories 75; Fat 6g; Sodium 111mg; Carbs 5.6g; Fiber 2.5g; Sugar 2.9g; Protein 2.8g

Spicy Gujarati Green Beans

Prep time: 5 minutes| Cook time: 10 minutes| Serves: 3

¾ pound fresh green beans, trimmed
1 garlic clove, minced
2 tablespoons olive oil
1 tablespoon soy sauce

1 teaspoon black mustard seeds
1 dried red chile pepper, crushed
Sea salt and ground black pepper, to taste

1. Select the "AIR FRY" function of Ninja Foodi Smart XL Pro Air Oven, set temperature to 380°F and time to 8 minutes. Select START/STOP to begin preheating. Toss the green beans with the remaining ingredients; then arrange them in the Air Fryer basket. 2. Slide basket into rails of Level 3, cook the green beans for 8 minutes, tossing the basket halfway through the cooking time. Enjoy!

Per Serving: Calories 136; Fat 9.8g; Sodium 239mg; Carbs 2.7g; Fiber 3.3g; Sugar 4.9g; Protein 2.7g

Mushroom Patties

Prep time: 5 minutes| Cook time: 15 minutes| Serves: 3

¾-pound brown mushrooms, chopped
1 large eggs, whisked
½ cup breadcrumbs
½ cup parmesan cheese, grated

1 small onion, minced
1 garlic clove, minced
Sea salt and ground black pepper, to taste
1 tablespoon olive oil

1. Slide basket into rails of Level 3. Select the "AIR FRY" function of Ninja Foodi Smart XL Pro Air Oven, set temperature to 380°F and time to 15 minutes. Select START/STOP to begin preheating. Mix all ingredients until everything is well combined. Form the mixture into three patties. 2. Place the basket in the air fryer, cook the burgers for about 15 minutes or until cooked through. Bon appétit!

Per Serving: Calories 184; Fat 11.1g; Sodium 332mg; Carbs 14g; Fiber 1.5g; Sugar 4g; Protein 9.4g

Chapter 3 Poultry

Cornish Game Hens with Thai Cucumber Salad

Prep time: 10 minutes.| Cooking time: 23 minutes. | Servings: 2

2 (1¼-pound) Cornish game hens, giblets discarded
6 tablespoons chopped fresh cilantro
2 tablespoons packed light brown sugar
1 tablespoon fish sauce
2 garlic cloves, minced
2 teaspoons grated lime zest
1 Thai chile, stemmed, seeded, and minced

1 tablespoon lime juice
2 teaspoons vegetable oil
1 teaspoon ground coriander
Black pepper and salt
1 English cucumber, halved lengthwise and sliced thin
1 small shallot, sliced thin
2 tablespoons chopped dry-roasted peanuts

1. lightly spray air-fryer basket with vegetable oil spray. To handle 1 hen at a time, cut along both sides of the hen's backbone with kitchen shears to remove it. Flatten hens and lay breast side up on counter. Using sharp chef's knife, cut through center of breast to make 2 halves. 2. Using your fingers, gently loosen skin covering breast and thighs. Pat hens dry with paper towels. Using metal skewer, poke 10 to 15 holes in fat deposits on top of breasts and thighs. Tuck wingtips underneath hens. 3. Mix ¼ cup cilantro, 4 teaspoons sugar, 2 teaspoons fish sauce, garlic, lime zest, 1 teaspoon oil, coriander, ½ teaspoon pepper, and ⅛ teaspoon salt in bowl. Rub cilantro mixture evenly under skin of hens and set aside to marinate for 10 minutes. 4. Spread hens breast side up in prepared basket. Insert its air fryer basket into the level 3 of the oven and close the door. Cook on Air Fry mode, set its temperature to400 degrees F/ 200 degrees C and set the time to23 minutes, rotating hens halfway through (do not flip). Transfer hens to a cutting board, bandage loosely with aluminum foil, and leave for 5 minutes. 5. Meanwhile, whisk lime juice, Thai chile, remaining 2 teaspoons sugar, remaining 1 teaspoon fish sauce, and remaining 1 teaspoon oil in medium serving bowl. Add cucumber, shallot, and remaining 2 tablespoons cilantro and toss to coat. Season with black pepper and salt to taste and sprinkle with peanuts. Serve hens with cucumber salad and lime wedges.
Per Serving: Calories 210; Fat 17.8g; Sodium 619mg; Carbs 21g; Fiber 1.4g; Sugar 1.8g; Protein 3.4g

Chicken Cheese Dinner Rolls

Prep time: 5 minutes| Cook time: 15 minutes| Serves: 4

1-pound chicken, ground
½ cup tortilla chips, crushed
2 ounces cheddar cheese, grated
1 teaspoon dried parsley flakes
1 teaspoon cayenne pepper

½ teaspoon paprika
Kosher salt
Ground black pepper
4 dinner rolls

1. Install the wire rack on Level 3. Select the "AIR ROAST" function of Ninja Foodi Smart XL Pro Air Oven, set temperature to 380°F and time to 17 minutes. Select START/STOP to begin preheating. Mix the chicken, tortilla chips, cheese, and spices until everything is well combined. Now, roll the mixture into four patties. 2. Cook the burgers for about 17 minutes or until cooked through; turn over halfway through the cooking time. 3. Serve your burgers in dinner rolls. Bon appétit!
Per Serving: Calories 575; Fat 25.3g; Sodium 369mg; Carbs 37g; Fiber 3.2g; Sugar 4.6g; Protein 49.7g

Chicken Cutlets with steamed Broccoli

Prep time: 5 minutes| Cook time: 15 minutes| Serves: 4

1-pound chicken cutlets
1-pound broccoli florets
1 tablespoon olive oil

Sea salt
Ground black pepper, to taste

1. Select Level 3. Select the "AIR FRY" function of Ninja Foodi Smart XL Pro Air Oven, set temperature to 380°F and time to 6 minutes. Select START/STOP to begin preheating. Pat the chicken dry with kitchen towels. Place the chicken cutlets in a lightly greased Air Fryer basket. 2. Cook the chicken cutlets for 6 minutes, turning them over halfway through the cooking time. 3. Turn the heat to 400 °F and add in the remaining ingredients. Continue to cook for 6 minutes more. Bon appétit!
Per Serving: Calories 313; Fat 20.8g; Sodium 444mg; Carbs 7.5g; Fiber 2g; Sugar 1.9g; Protein 24.5g

Chicken Lettuce Wraps

Prep time: 10 minutes.| Cooking time: 12 minutes. | Servings: 4

1 pound boneless, skinless chicken thighs, trimmed
1 teaspoon vegetable oil
2 tablespoons lime juice
1 shallot, minced
1 tablespoon fish sauce, plus extra for serving
2 teaspoons packed brown sugar
1 garlic clove, minced
⅛ teaspoon red pepper flakes

1 mango, peeled, and diced
⅓ cup chopped fresh mint
⅓ cup chopped fresh cilantro
⅓ cup chopped fresh Thai basil
1 head bibb lettuce (8 ounces), leaves separated
¼ cup dry-roasted peanuts, chopped
2 Thai chiles, stemmed and sliced thin

1. Pat the boneless chicken dry with paper towels and rub liberally with oil. Place chicken in air-fryer basket. Insert its air fryer basket into the level 3 of the oven and close the door. set its temperature to 400 degrees F/ 200 degrees C. Cook until chicken registers 175 degrees, for 12 to 16 minutes on "Air Fry" Mode. Flip once cooked half way through. 2. Meanwhile, whisk lime juice, shallot, fish sauce, sugar, garlic, and pepper flakes in large bowl; set aside. 3. Transfer the cooked chicken to a cutting board, cool slightly, and use two forks to cut it into bite-sized pieces. Add shredded chicken, mango, mint, cilantro, and basil to bowl with dressing and toss to coat. Serve chicken in lettuce leaves, passing peanuts, Thai chiles, and extra fish sauce separately.

Per Serving: Calories 398; Fat 37.8 g; Sodium 1463 mg; Carbs 2.5g; Fiber 0.2g; Sugar 0.5g; Protein 13.6g

Spicy Chicken Drumsticks

Prep time: 10 minutes.| Cooking time: 22 minutes. | Servings: 2

2 teaspoons paprika
1 teaspoon packed brown sugar
1 teaspoon garlic powder
½ teaspoon dry mustard
½ teaspoon salt

Pinch pepper
4 (5-ounce) chicken drumsticks, trimmed
1 teaspoon vegetable oil
1 scallion, sliced

1. Mix paprika, sugar, garlic powder, mustard, salt, and pepper in bowl. Pat drumsticks dry with paper towels. Using metal skewer, poke 10 to 15 holes in skin of each drumstick. Rub liberally with oil and sprinkle evenly with spice mixture. 2. Spread drumsticks in air-fryer basket, spaced evenly apart, alternating ends. Insert its air fryer basket into the level 3 of the oven and close the door. set its temperature to400 degrees F/ 200 degrees C. Cook for 25 minutes on "Air Fry" mode, flipping and rotating chicken halfway through, until chicken is crisp. 3. Transfer the prepared chicken to serving platter and let rest for 5 minutes. Sprinkle with scallion. Serve.

Per Serving: Calories 267; Fat 15.2 g; Sodium 479 mg; Carbs 13.9g; Fiber 0.1g; Sugar 12.9g; Protein 20.6g

Turkey and Spinach

Prep time: 5 minutes. | Cooking time: 15 minutes. | Servings: 4

1-pound turkey meat, ground and browned
1 tablespoon garlic, minced
1 tablespoon ginger, grated

2 tablespoons coconut aminos
4 cups spinach leaves
A pinch of black pepper and salt

1. In a suitable pan that fits your air fryer, mix all the recipe ingredients and toss. 2. Put the pan in its air fryer basket. Insert its air fryer basket into the level 3 of the oven and close the door. Cook on "Air Fry" Mode, select level 3, and set its temperature to 380 degrees F/ 195 degrees C for 15 minutes divide everything into bowls and serve.

Per Serving: Calories 116; Fat 2.3 g; Sodium 15 mg; Carbs 18.9g; Fiber 4.5g; Sugar 2.2g; Protein 6g

Jerk Chicken

Prep time: 10 minutes.| Cooking time: 27 minutes. | Servings: 2

1 tablespoon packed brown sugar
1 teaspoon ground allspice
1 teaspoon pepper
1 teaspoon garlic powder
¾ teaspoon dry mustard
¾ teaspoon dried thyme

½ teaspoon salt
¼ teaspoon cayenne pepper
2 (10-ounce) chicken leg quarters, trimmed
1 teaspoon vegetable oil
1 scallion, green part only, sliced thin
Lime wedges

1. Mix sugar, allspice, pepper, garlic powder, mustard, thyme, salt, and cayenne in bowl. Pat chicken dry with paper towels. Using metal skewer, poke 10 to 15 holes in skin of each chicken leg. Rub liberally with oil and sprinkle evenly with spice mixture.2. Spread chicken skin side up in air-fryer basket, spaced evenly apart. Cook on Air Fry mode. Insert its air fryer basket into the level 3 of the oven and close the door. set its temperature to400 degrees F/ 200 degrees C and set the time to 27 minutes. Cook until chicken is well browned and crisp and registers 195 degrees, 27 to 30 minutes, rotating chicken halfway through.3. Transfer the prepared chicken to plate, tent loosely with aluminum foil, and let rest for 5 minutes. Sprinkle with scallion. Serve with lime wedges.

Per Serving: Calories 368; Fat 32.8 g; Sodium 507 mg; Carbs 0.6g; Fiber 0.1g; Sugar 1.1g; Protein 18.5g

Spicy Chicken Drumsticks with Cheese

Prep time: 10 minutes.| Cooking time: 22 minutes. | Servings: 2

1½ teaspoons paprika
½ teaspoon cayenne pepper
¼ teaspoon salt
¼ teaspoon pepper
4 (5-ounce) chicken drumsticks, trimmed
1 teaspoon vegetable oil

3 tablespoons hot sauce
2 tablespoons unsalted butter
2 teaspoons molasses
¼ teaspoon cornstarch
2 tablespoons crumbled blue cheese

1. Mix paprika, cayenne, salt, and pepper in bowl. Pat drumsticks dry with paper towels. Using metal skewer, poke 10 to 15 holes in skin of each drumstick. Rub liberally with oil and sprinkle evenly with spice mixture. 2. Spread drumsticks in air-fryer basket, spaced evenly apart, alternating ends. Insert its air fryer basket into the level 3 of the oven and close the door. set its temperature to 400 degrees F/ 200 degrees C. Cook on Air Fry mode for 22 to 25 minutes, flipping chicken halfway through. Transfer the prepared chicken to large plate, tent loosely with aluminum foil, and let rest for 5 minutes. 3. Meanwhile, microwave hot sauce, butter, molasses, and cornstarch in large bowl, stirring occasionally, until hot, about 1 minute. Add chicken and toss to coat. Transfer to serving platter and sprinkle with blue cheese. Serve.

Per Serving: Calories 257; Fat 17 g; Sodium 674 mg; Carbs 13.9g; Fiber 4.2; Sugar 5.9g; Protein 13.6g

Ricotta Adobo Chicken

Prep time: 15 minutes. | Cooking time: 18 minutes. | Servings: 3

3 chicken thighs, boneless
2 teaspoons adobo sauce
1 teaspoon ricotta cheese

1 teaspoon dried thyme
cooking spray

1. In the mixing bowl mix up adobo sauce and ricotta cheese, then add dried thyme and churn the mixture. 2. Then brush the chicken thighs with adobo sauce mixture and leave for 10 minutes to marinate. 3. Select the Air Fry mode. Set the Ninja Foodi Smart XL Pro temperature to385 degrees F/ 195 degrees C. Select Level "3" and set the time on your Ninja Foodi Smart XL Pro Air Fryer Oven to 18 minutes. Press Start/Pause to begin preheating. Continue to the next step when it is done preheating. 4. Spray its air fryer basket with cooking spray and put the chicken thighs inside. 5. Insert its air fryer basket into the level 3 of the oven and close the door. Cook them for 18 minutes.

Per Serving: Calories 398; Fat 27 g; Sodium 416mg; Carbs 34.9g; Fiber 6.5g; Sugar 6.9g; Protein 11.6g

Turkey Cheese Burgers

Prep time: 10 minutes.| Cooking time: 12 minutes. | Servings: 2

½ slice sandwich bread, torn into ½-inch pieces
2 tablespoons plain yogurt
Black pepper and salt
8 ounces ground turkey

1 ounce Monterey jack cheese, shredded (¼ cup)
2 hamburger buns, toasted if desired
½ tomato, sliced thin
1 cup baby arugula

1. Mash bread, yogurt, ¼ teaspoon salt, and ¼ teaspoon pepper to paste in medium bowl using fork. Break up ground turkey into small pieces over bread mixture in bowl, then add Monterey jack, and lightly knead with hands until mixture forms cohesive mass. 2. Divide turkey mixture into 2 lightly packed balls, then gently flatten each into 1-inch-thick patty. Press center of each patty with your fingertips to create ¼-inch-deep depression. Season with black pepper and salt. 3. Spread patties in air-fryer basket, spaced evenly apart. Cook on Air Fry mode. Insert its air fryer basket into the level 3 of the oven and close the door. Set its temperature to 350 degrees F/ 175 degrees C and set the time to 12 minutes. Cook until burgers are browned and register 160 degrees F/70 degree C, 12 to 16 minutes, flipping and rotating burgers halfway through. 4. Transfer burgers to large plate, tent loosely with aluminum foil, and let rest for 5 minutes. 5. Serve.

Per Serving: Calories 341; Fat 24.6 g; Sodium 401 mg; Carbs 12g; Fiber 0.1g; Sugar 11.9g; Protein 18.6g

Tandoori Chicken

Prep time: 10 minutes.| Cooking time: 20 minutes. | Servings: 2

3 garlic cloves, minced
1 tablespoon grated fresh ginger
1½ teaspoons garam masala
1 teaspoon ground cumin
1 teaspoon chili powder

1 teaspoon vegetable oil
Black pepper and salt
½ cup plain whole-milk yogurt
4 teaspoons lime juice
4 (5-ounce) bone-in chicken thighs, trimmed

1. Mix garlic, ginger, garam masala, cumin, chili powder, oil, ¼ teaspoon salt, and ¼ teaspoon pepper in large bowl and microwave, about 30 seconds. Set aside to cool slightly, then stir in ¼ cup yogurt and 1 tablespoon lime juice. 2. Pat chicken dry with paper towels. Using metal skewer, poke skin side of chicken 10 to 15 times. Add to bowl with yogurt-spice mixture and toss to coat; set aside to marinate for 10 minutes. Meanwhile, mix remaining ¼ cup yogurt and remaining 1 teaspoon lime juice in clean bowl; season with black pepper and salt to taste and set aside. 3. Remove the marinated chicken from marinade and let the excess drip off, and spread skin side up in air-fryer basket, spaced evenly apart. Cook on Air Fry mode. Insert its air fryer basket into the level 3 of the oven and close the door. Set its temperature to400 degrees F/ 200 degrees C and set the time to 20 minutes. Cook until chicken is well browned and crisp, 20 to 30 minutes, rotating chicken halfway through. 4. Transfer the prepared chicken to serving platter, tent loosely with aluminum foil, and let rest for 5 minutes. Serve with reserved yogurt-lime sauce.

Per Serving: Calories 382; Fat 32.5 g; Sodium 1363 mg; Carbs 3.2g; Fiber 0.2g; Sugar 1.9g; Protein 19.1g

Buttery Turkey with Mushroom

Prep time: 5 minutes. | Cooking time: 25 minutes. | Servings: 4

6 cups leftover turkey meat, skinless, boneless and shredded
A pinch of black pepper and salt
1 tablespoon parsley, chopped
1 cup chicken stock

3 tablespoons butter, melted
1 pound mushrooms, sliced
2 spring onions, chopped

1. Heat up a suitable pan that fits the air fryer with the butter over medium-high heat, then add the mushrooms and sauté for about 5 minutes. 2. Add the rest of the recipe ingredients, toss, put the pan in the machine. 3. Insert its air fryer basket into the level 3 of the oven and close the door. Cook on "Air Fry" Mode, select level 3, and set its temperature to 370 degrees F/ 185 degrees C for 20 minutes. Divide everything between plates and serve.

Per Serving: Calories 324; Fat 17.8 g; Sodium 363 mg; Carbs 8.9g; Fiber 0.5g; Sugar 1.9g; Protein 36.6g

Turkey Meatloaves

Prep time: 10 minutes. | Cooking time: 25 minutes. | Servings: 2

1 shallot, minced
1 tablespoon vegetable oil
1 garlic clove, minced
½ teaspoon minced fresh thyme or ⅛ teaspoon dried
Pinch cayenne pepper
1 slice white sandwich bread, torn into ½-inch pieces
1 large egg, lightly beaten
1 tablespoon whole milk

1 tablespoon Worcestershire sauce
¼ teaspoon salt
¼ teaspoon pepper
1-pound ground turkey
¼ cup ketchup
1 tablespoon cider vinegar
1 tablespoon packed brown sugar
½ teaspoon hot sauce

1. Fold 1 long sheet of aluminum foil into a 4-inch wide sling to use with the air fryer basket. Lay a layer of foil across the basket widthwise, pressing it into the bottom and up the sides. If necessary, fold any extra foil so that the edges are flush with the top of the basket. Spray foil and the basket with vegetable oil spray sparingly. 2. Microwave shallot, oil, garlic, thyme, and cayenne in large bowl until fragrant, about 1 minute. Add bread, egg, milk, Worcestershire, salt, and pepper and mash mixture to paste using fork. Break up ground turkey into small pieces over bread mixture and knead with hands until well mixed. Shape turkey mixture into two 5 by 3-inch loaves. Spread loaves on sling in prepared basket, spaced evenly apart. 3. Mix ketchup, vinegar, sugar, and hot sauce in small bowl, then brush loaves with half of ketchup mixture. Cook on Air Fry mode. Insert its air fryer basket into the level 3 of the oven and close the door. set its temperature to 350 degrees. Cook until meatloaves register 160 degrees, 25 to 30 minutes, brushing with remaining ketchup mixture and rotating meatloaves using sling halfway through. 4. Using foil sling, carefully remove meatloaves from basket. Serve.

Per Serving: Calories 634; Fat 19.6 g; Sodium 1263 mg; Carbs 13.1g; Fiber 1.5g; Sugar 8.6g; Protein 96g

Tasty Thyme Chicken Breast

Prep time: 10 minutes. | Cooking time: 17 minutes. | Servings: 3

1-pound chicken breast, skinless, boneless
1 teaspoon garlic powder
1 teaspoon dried thyme
1 teaspoon salt

½ teaspoon black pepper
½ teaspoon cayenne pepper
2 teaspoons sunflower oil

1. Sprinkle the chicken breast with garlic powder, dried thyme, salt, black pepper, and cayenne pepper. 2. Then gently brush the chicken with sunflower oil and put it in the air fryer. Cook on Air Fry mode. Insert its air fryer basket into the level 3 of the oven and close the door. Set the time on your Ninja Foodi Smart XL Pro Air Fryer Oven to 17 minutes. Slice the cooked chicken into Servings.

Per Serving: Calories 213; Fat 4.1 g; Sodium 303 mg; Carbs 37.9g; Fiber 1.5g; Sugar 1.9g; Protein 6.6g

Buttery Chicken Wings

Prep time: 5 minutes| Cook time: 15 minutes| Serves: 2

¾-pound chicken wings, boneless
1 tablespoon butter, room temperature
½ teaspoon garlic powder

½ teaspoon shallot powder
½ teaspoon mustard powder

1. Select Level 3. Select the "AIR FRY" function of Ninja Foodi Smart XL Pro Air Oven, set temperature to 380°F and time to 18 minutes. Select START/STOP to begin preheating. Toss the chicken wings with the remaining ingredients. 2. Cook the chicken wings for 18 minutes, turning them over halfway through the cooking time.

Per Serving: Calories 265; Fat 11.7g; Sodium 322mg; Carbs 0.5g; Fiber 0.9g; Sugar 0.5g; Protein 37.5g

Turkey and Asparagus

Prep time: 5 minutes. | Cooking time: 25 minutes. | Servings: 4

1-pound turkey breast soft loins, cut into strips
1-pound asparagus, trimmed and cut into medium pieces
A pinch of black pepper and salt
1 tablespoon lemon juice

1 teaspoon coconut aminos
2 tablespoons olive oil
2 garlic cloves, minced
¼ cup chicken stock

1. Heat up a suitable pan that fits the air fryer with the oil over medium-high heat, then add the meat and brown for 2 minutes per side. 2. Add the rest of the recipe ingredients, toss, put the pan in the machine. Insert its air fryer basket into the level 3 of the oven and close the door. Cook on "Air Fry" Mode, select level 3, and set its temperature to 380 degrees F/ 195 degrees C for 20 minutes. 3. Divide everything between plates and serve

Per Serving: Calories 249; Fat 5.7 g; Sodium 574 mg; Carbs 23.9g; Fiber 0.9g; Sugar 1.9g; Protein 3.6g

Lemongrass Chicken Breast

Prep time: 25 minutes. | Cooking time: 20 minutes. | Servings: 5

15 ounces chicken breast, skinless, boneless
1 teaspoon lemongrass
1 teaspoon black pepper
1 teaspoon salt
1 teaspoon chili powder
1 teaspoon smoked paprika
2 teaspoons apple cider vinegar

1 teaspoon lemon juice
1 tablespoon sunflower oil
1 teaspoon dried basil
½ teaspoon ground coriander
2 tablespoons water
1 tablespoon heavy cream

1. Make the marinade: in the bowl mix up lemongrass, black pepper, salt, chili powder, smoked paprika, apple cider vinegar, lemon juice, sunflower oil, dried basil, ground coriander, water, and heavy cream. 2. Then chop the chicken breast roughly and put it in the marinade. Stir it well and leave for 20 minutes in the fridge. 3. Then Select the Air Fry mode. Set the Ninja Foodi Smart XL Pro temperature to 375 degrees F/ 190 degrees C. Select Level "3" and set the time on your Ninja Foodi Smart XL Pro Air Fryer Oven to 20 minutes. Press Start/Pause to begin preheating. Continue to the next step when it is done preheating. 4. Put the marinated chicken breast pieces in the air fryer. Insert its air fryer basket into the level 3 of the oven and close the door. and cook them for 20 minutes. Shake the chicken pieces after 10 minutes of cooking to avoid burning. 5.The cooked chicken breast pieces should have a light brown color.

Per Serving: Calories 351; Fat 20.3 g; Sodium 298 mg; Carbs 40.9g; Fiber 0.5g; Sugar 35.5g; Protein3.6g

Mascarpone Chicken Fillets

Prep time: 15 minutes. | Cooking time: 12 minutes. | Servings: 4

1 tablespoon fresh basil, chopped
4 ounces mozzarella, sliced
12 ounces chicken fillet

1 tablespoon nut oil
1 teaspoon chili flakes
1 teaspoon mascarpone

1. Brush the air fryer pan with nut oil. Then cut the chicken fillet on 4 Servings and beat them gently with a kitchen hammer. 2. After this, sprinkle the chicken fillets with chili flakes and put in the air fryer pan in one layer. Top the fillets with fresh basil and sprinkle with mascarpone. 3. After this, top the chicken fillets with sliced mozzarella. 4. Select the Air Fry mode. Set the Ninja Foodi Smart XL Pro temperature to 375 degrees F/ 190 degrees C. Select Level "3" and set the time on your Ninja Foodi Smart XL Pro Air Fryer Oven to 12 minutes. 5. Put the pan with caprese chicken fillets in its air fryer basket. Insert its air fryer basket into the level 3 of the oven and close the door. Cook them for 12 minutes.

Per Serving: Calories 386; Fat 10.3 g; Sodium 238 mg; Carbs 72.9g; Fiber 4.5g; Sugar 59g; Protein 2.6g

Ground Turkey with Green Beans

Prep time: 5 minutes. | Cooking time: 25 minutes. | Servings: 4

1-pound turkey meat, ground
A pinch of black pepper and salt
2 tablespoons olive oil

2 teaspoons parsley flakes
1 pound green beans, trimmed and halved
2 teaspoons garlic powder

1. Heat up a suitable pan that fits the air fryer with the oil over medium-high heat, then add the meat and brown it for 5 minutes. 2. Add the remaining recipe ingredients, toss, put the pan in the machine. Insert its air fryer basket into the level 3 of the oven and close the door. and Cook on "Air Fry" Mode, select level 3, and set its temperature to 370 degrees F/ 185 degrees C for 20 minutes. 3. Divide between plates and serve.

Per Serving: Calories 416; Fat 8.3 g; Sodium 208 mg; Carbs 22.9g; Fiber 0.5g; Sugar 19g; Protein 60.6g

Ground Turkey with Cabbage

Prep time: 5 minutes. | Cooking time: 25 minutes. | Servings: 4

1-pound turkey meat, ground
A pinch of black pepper and salt
2 tablespoons butter, melted
1-ounce chicken stock

1 small red cabbage head, shredded
1 tablespoon sweet paprika, chopped
1 tablespoon parsley, chopped

1. Heat up a suitable pan that fits the air fryer with the butter, then add the meat and brown for 5 minutes. 2. Add all the other ingredients, toss, put the pan in its air fryer basket. Insert its air fryer basket into the level 3 of the oven and close the door. Cook on "Air Fry" Mode, select level 3, and set its temperature to 380 degrees F/ 195 degrees C for 20 minutes. Divide everything between plates and serve.

Per Serving: Calories 426; Fat 36.3 g; Sodium 248 mg; Carbs 22.1g; Fiber 2g; Sugar 10.9g; Protein 6.6g

Country Chicken Tenders

Prep time: 5 minutes| Cook time: 15 minutes| Serves: 4

¾ lb. of chicken tenders
For breading:
2 tablespoons olive oil
1 teaspoon black pepper
½ teaspoon salt

½ cup seasoned breadcrumbs
½ cup all-purpose flour
2 eggs, beaten

1. Select Level 3. Select the "AIR FRY" function of Ninja Foodi Smart XL Pro Air Oven, set temperature to 330°F and time to 10 minutes. Select START/STOP to begin preheating. 2. In three separate bowls, set aside breadcrumbs, eggs, and flour. Season the breadcrumbs with salt and pepper. Add olive oil to the breadcrumbs and mix well. 3. Place chicken tenders into flour, then dip into eggs and finally dip into breadcrumbs. Press to ensure that the breadcrumbs are evenly coating the chicken. Shake off excess breading and place in the air fryer basket. Cook the chicken tenders for 10-minutes in the air fryer. Serve warm.

Per Serving: Calories 271; Fat 9.3g; Sodium 15mg; Carbs 43g; Fiber 6g; Sugar 2g; Protein 5g

Cheesy Turkey Cubes

Prep time: 5 minutes. | Cooking time: 20 minutes. | Servings: 4

1 big turkey breast, skinless, boneless and cubed
Black pepper and salt to the taste
¼ cup cheddar cheese, grated

¼ teaspoon garlic powder
1 tablespoon olive oil

1. Rub the turkey cubes with the oil, season with salt, pepper and garlic powder and dredge in cheddar cheese. 2. Put the turkey bits in your air fryer's basket. Insert its air fryer basket into the level 3 of the oven and close the door. And Cook on "Air Fry" Mode, select level 3, and set its temperature to 380 degrees F/ 195 degrees C for 20 minutes. Divide between plates and serve with a side salad.

Per Serving: Calories 477; Fat 13.3 g; Sodium 128 mg; Carbs 89.5g; Fiber 6.5g; Sugar 59.2g; Protein 5.4g

Spicy Marinated Chicken

Prep time: 10 minutes| Cook time: 15 minutes| Serves: 2

¾-pound chicken breasts, boneless, skinless
1 teaspoon garlic, minced
½ cup red wine

¼ cup hot sauce
1 tablespoon Dijon mustard
Sea salt and cayenne pepper, to taste

1. Select Level 3. Select the "AIR FRY" function of Ninja Foodi Smart XL Pro Air Oven, set temperature to 380°F and time to 12 minutes. Select START/STOP to begin preheating. Place the chicken, garlic, red wine, hot sauce, and mustard in a ceramic bowl. Cover and let it marinate for about 3 hours in your refrigerator. 2. Place the chicken in the Air Fryer basket. 3. Cook the chicken breasts for 12 minutes, turning them over halfway through the cooking time. 4. Spice it with the salt and cayenne pepper to taste. Bon appétit!

Per Serving: Calories 313; Fat 16g; Sodium 542mg; Carbs 3.7g; Fiber 0.9g; Sugar 2g; Protein 36.5g

Herbed Turkey Drumsticks

Prep time: 10 minutes| Cook time: 45 minutes| Serves: 5

2 pounds turkey drumsticks, bone-in
2 tablespoons olive oil
Kosher salt
Ground black pepper, to taste

1 teaspoon dried thyme
1 teaspoon dried rosemary
1 teaspoon garlic, minced

1. Select Level 3. Select the "AIR FRY" function of Ninja Foodi Smart XL Pro Air Oven, set temperature to 400°F and time to 40 minutes. Select START/STOP to begin preheating. Toss the turkey drumsticks with the remaining ingredients. 2. Cook the turkey drumsticks for 40 minutes, turning them over halfway through the cooking time. Bon appétit!

Per Serving: Calories 341; Fat 21.7g; Sodium 324mg; Carbs 0.5g; Fiber 0.1g; Sugar 0.1g; Protein 35.5g

Tangy Ranch Chicken Wings

Prep time: 10 minutes| Cook time: 25 minutes| Serves: 3

1-pound chicken wings, boneless
2 tablespoons olive oil
1 teaspoon Ranch seasoning mix

Kosher salt
Ground black pepper

1. Select Level 3. Select the "AIR FRY" function of Ninja Foodi Smart XL Pro Air Oven, set temperature to 380°F and time to 22 minutes. Select START/STOP to begin preheating. Pat the chicken dry with kitchen towels. Toss the chicken with the remaining ingredients. 2. Cook the chicken wings for 22 minutes, turning them over halfway through the cooking time. Bon appétit!

Per Serving: Calories 273; Fat14.3g; Sodium 357mg; Carbs 0.5g; Fiber 0.5g; Sugar 0.4g; Protein 33.2g

Fried Chicken with Thyme

Prep time: 20 minutes. | Cooking time: 75 minutes. | Servings: 4

16 ounces whole chicken
1 tablespoon dried thyme
1 teaspoon ground cumin

1 teaspoon salt
1 tablespoon avocado oil

1. Cut the chicken into halves and sprinkle it with dried thyme, cumin, and salt. Then brush the chicken halves with avocado oil. 2. Select the Air Fry mode. Set the Ninja Foodi Smart XL Pro temperature to 365 degrees F/ 185 degrees C. Select Level "3" and set the time on your Ninja Foodi Smart XL Pro Air Fryer Oven to 60 minutes. Press Start/Pause to begin preheating. Continue to the next step when it is done preheating. 3. Put the chicken halves in its air fryer basket. Insert its air fryer basket into the level 3 of the oven and close the door. Cook them for 60 minutes. 4. Then flip the chicken halves on another side and cook them for 15 minutes more.

Per Serving: Calories 148; Fat 0.3 g; Sodium 3 mg; Carbs 38.9g; Fiber 0.5g; Sugar 33.9g; Protein 0.6g

Cheesy Fried Chicken

Prep time: 10 minutes| Cook time: 20 minutes| Serves: 4

1 egg, whisked
½ cup parmesan cheese, preferably freshly grated
½ cup tortilla chips, crushed
½ teaspoon onion powder

½ teaspoon garlic powder
1 teaspoon red chili powder
1 ½ pounds chicken breasts, boneless skinless cut into strips

1. Install the wire rack on Level 3. Select the "AIR ROAST" function of Ninja Foodi Smart XL Pro Air Oven, set temperature to 380°F and time to 12 minutes. Select START/STOP to begin preheating. Whisk the egg in a shallow bowl. In a separate bowl, whisk the parmesan cheese, tortilla chips, onion powder, garlic powder, and red chili powder. 2. Dip the chicken into the egg mixture. Then, roll the chicken pieces over the cheese mixture. 3. Cook the chicken for 12 minutes, turning them over halfway through the cooking time. Bon appétit!

Per Serving: Calories 427; Fat 23.1g; Sodium 633mg; Carbs 11.1g; Fiber 0.9g; Sugar 0.6g; Protein 41.4g

Easy Turkey Schnitzel

Prep time: 10 minutes| Cook time: 25 minutes| Serves: 3

1½ pounds turkey thighs, skinless, boneless
1 egg, beaten
½ cup all-purpose flour
½ cup seasoned breadcrumbs

½ teaspoon red pepper flakes, crushed
Sea salt
Ground black pepper, to taste
1 tablespoon olive oil

1. Select Level 3. Select the "AIR FRY" function of Ninja Foodi Smart XL Pro Air Oven, set temperature to 380°F and time to 22 minutes. Select START/STOP to begin preheating. Flatten the turkey thighs with a mallet. 2. Whisk the egg in a bowl. Place the flour in another bowl. 3. Then, place the breadcrumbs, red pepper, salt, and black pepper in another bowl. Dip in the flour, then, in the egg, and roll them in the breadcrumb mixture. 4. Place the breaded turkey thighs in the Air Fryer basket. Mist your schnitzel with the olive oil and transfer them to the basket. 5. Cook the schnitzel for 22 minutes, turning them over halfway through the cooking time. Bon appétit!

Per Serving: Calories 579; Fat 27.4g; Sodium 456mg; Carbs 30.3g; Fiber 1.6g; Sugar 2g; Protein 51g

Peppery Chicken Fillets

Prep time: 10 minutes| Cook time: 20 minutes| Serves: 4

1-pound chicken fillets
2 tablespoons butter
2 bell peppers, seeded and sliced
1 teaspoon garlic, minced

Sea salt
Ground black pepper, to taste
1 teaspoon red pepper flakes

1. Install the wire rack on Level 3. Select the "AIR ROAST" function of Ninja Foodi Smart XL Pro Air Oven, set temperature to 380°F and time to 15 minutes. Select START/STOP to begin preheating. Toss the chicken fillets with the butter and place them in the Air Fryer basket. Top the chicken with bell peppers, garlic, salt, black pepper, and red pepper flakes. 2. Cook the chicken and peppers for 15 minutes, tossing the basket halfway through the cooking time. Serve warm and enjoy!

Per Serving: Calories 305; Fat 22.8g; Sodium 642mg; Carbs 2.3g; Fiber 0.4g; Sugar 1.1g; Protein 21.6g

Orange Duck

Prep time: 15 minutes| Cook time: 45 minutes| Serves: 4

1-pound duck legs
¼ cup orange sauce

Sea salt and red pepper flakes, crushed

1. Install the wire rack on Level 3. Select the "AIR ROAST" function of Ninja Foodi Smart XL Pro Air Oven, set temperature to 400°F and time to 40 minutes. Select START/STOP to begin preheating. Toss the duck legs with the remaining ingredients. 2. Cook the duck legs for 40 minutes, turning them over halfway through the cooking time. Bon appétit!

Per Serving: Calories 471; Fat 44.1g; Sodium 311mg; Carbs 2.9g; Fiber 0.3g; Sugar 2.1g; Protein 13.1g

Lemon Turkey with Parsley

Prep time: 10 minutes| Cook time: 40 minutes| Serves: 5

2 pounds turkey wings
2 tablespoons olive oil
½ teaspoon garlic powder
½ teaspoon onion powder

1 teaspoon poultry seasoning mix
2 tablespoons fresh parsley, roughly chopped
1 lemon, cut into slices

1. Select Level 3. Select the "AIR FRY" function of Ninja Foodi Smart XL Pro Air Oven, set temperature to 400°F and time to 40 minutes. Select START/STOP to begin preheating. Toss the turkey wings with olive oil, garlic powder, onion powder, and poultry seasoning mix. 2. Cook the turkey wings for 40 minutes, turning them over halfway through the cooking time. 3. Let it rest for 10 minutes before carving and serving. Garnish the turkey wings with the parsley and lemon slices. Bon appétit!

Per Serving: Calories 411; Fat 27.8g; Sodium 411mg; Carbs 1.3g; Fiber 0.2g; Sugar 0.3g; Protein 36.5g

Roasted Turkey with Scallions

Prep time: 10 minutes| Cook time: 40 minutes| Serves: 4

1½ pounds turkey legs
1 tablespoon butter, melted
1 teaspoon hot paprika
1 teaspoon garlic, pressed

Sea salt
Ground black pepper
2 tablespoons scallions, chopped

1. Install the wire rack on Level 3. Select the "AIR ROAST" function of Ninja Foodi Smart XL Pro Air Oven, set temperature to 400°F and time to 40 minutes. Select START/STOP to begin preheating. Toss the turkey legs with the remaining ingredients, except for the scallions. 2. Cook the turkey legs for 40 minutes, turning them over halfway through the cooking time. 3. Garnish the roasted turkey legs with the fresh scallions and enjoy!

Per Serving: Calories 279; Fat 14.4g; Sodium 678mg; Carbs 1.8g; Fiber 0.5g; Sugar 0.7g; Protein 33.6g

Teriyaki Chicken

Prep time: 10 minutes.| Cooking time: 27 minutes. | Servings: 2

¼ cup chicken broth
1½ tablespoons soy sauce
½ teaspoon grated fresh ginger
⅛ teaspoon red pepper flakes
4 (5-ounce) bone-in chicken thighs, trimmed
1 tablespoon sugar
1 tablespoon mirin

½ teaspoon cornstarch
6 ounces snow peas, strings removed
1 garlic clove, minced
⅛ teaspoon grated lemon zest plus ½ teaspoon juice
¼ teaspoon salt
Pinch pepper

1. Whisk broth, soy sauce, ginger, and pepper flakes in large bowl. Pat chicken dry with paper towels. Using metal skewer, poke skin side of chicken 10 to 15 times. Add to bowl with broth mixture and toss to coat; set aside to marinate for 10 minutes. 2. Remove chicken from marinade and pat dry with paper towels. Measure out 2 tablespoons remaining marinade and mix with sugar, mirin, and cornstarch in bowl; discard remainder. Microwave, stirring occasionally, until thickened and bubbling, about 1 minute; set aside. 3. Spread chicken skin side up in air-fryer basket, spaced evenly apart. Cook on Air Fry mode, insert its air fryer basket into the level 3 of the oven and close the door. and set its temperature to 400 degrees F/ 200 degrees C and set the time to 20 minutes. Cook until chicken is golden, crisp, and registers 195 degrees, 20 to 25 minutes, rotating chicken halfway through (do not flip). Brush chicken skin with thickened marinade mixture. Return basket to air fryer oven and cook until chicken is well browned, about 5 minutes. Transfer the prepared chicken to serving platter, cover with aluminum foil, and let rest for 5 minutes. Measure out ½ teaspoon fat from air-fryer drawer; discard remainder. 4. While chicken rests, toss reserved fat, snow peas, garlic, lemon zest, salt, and pepper in bowl and transfer to now-empty basket. Insert its air fryer basket into the level 3 of the oven and close the door. cook until snow peas are crisp-soft, 2 to 3 minutes. Transfer to serving bowl and toss with lemon juice. Serve with chicken.

Per Serving: Calories 396 ; Fat 23.2g; Sodium 622mg; Carbs 0.7g; Fiber 0g; Sugar 0g; Protein 5.6g

Turkey and Avocado Sliders

Prep time: 10 minutes| Cook time: 25 minutes| Serves: 4

1-pound turkey, ground
1 tablespoon olive oil
1 avocado, peeled, pitted and chopped
2 garlic cloves, minced

½ cup breadcrumbs
Kosher salt
Ground black pepper
8 small rolls

1. Select Level 3. Select the "AIR FRY" function of Ninja Foodi Smart XL Pro Air Oven, set temperature to 380°F and time to 20 minutes. Select START/STOP to begin preheating. Mix the turkey, olive oil, avocado, garlic, breadcrumbs, salt, and black pepper until everything is well combined. Form the mixture into eight small patties. 2. Cook the patties for about 20 minutes or until cooked through; turn over halfway through the cooking time.3.Serve your patties in the prepared rolls and enjoy!

Per Serving: Calories 519; Fat 22.4g; Sodium 711mg; Carbs 48g; Fiber 5g; Sugar 6.7g; Protein 31.6g

Creamy Chicken Salad

Prep time: 5 minutes| Cook time: 20 minutes| Serves: 4

1-pound chicken breasts, skinless and boneless
¼ cup mayonnaise
¼ cup sour cream

1 tablespoon lemon juice
Sea salt and ground black pepper
½ cup celery, chopped

1. Select Level 3. Select the "AIR FRY" function of Ninja Foodi Smart XL Pro Air Oven, set temperature to 380°F and time to 5 minutes. Select START/STOP to begin preheating. Pat dry the chicken and place the chicken in a lightly oiled air fryer basket. 2. Cook the chicken breasts for 12 minutes, turning them over halfway through the cooking time.3.Shred the chicken breasts using two forks; transfer it to a salad bowl and add in the remaining ingredients.4.Toss to combine and serve well chilled. Bon appétit!

Per Serving: Calories 315; Fat 23g; Sodium 478mg; Carbs 2.8g; Fiber 0.4g; Sugar 0.9g; Protein 24.5g

Tasty Chicken Salad Sandwich

Prep time: 10 minutes| Cook time: 20 minutes| Serves: 4

1-pound chicken breasts, boneless and skinless
1 stalks celery, chopped
1 carrot, chopped
1 small onion, chopped

1 cup mayonnaise
Sea salt
Ground black pepper, to taste
4 sandwich buns

1. Select Level 3. Select the "AIR FRY" function of Ninja Foodi Smart XL Pro Air Oven, set temperature to 380°F and time to 12 minutes. Select START/STOP to begin preheating. Pat dry the chicken and place the chicken in a lightly oiled basket. 2. Cook the chicken breasts for 12 minutes, turning them over halfway through the cooking time. 3. Shred the chicken breasts using two forks; transfer it to a salad bowl and add in the celery, carrot, onion, mayo, salt, and pepper. 4. Toss to combine and serve in sandwich buns. Enjoy!

Per Serving: Calories 522; Fat 31.4g; Sodium 478mg; Carbs 27.1g; Fiber 2.5g; Sugar 5.2g; Protein 31.6g

Cheesy Ham Stuffed Chicken

Prep time: 5 minutes| Cook time: 22 minutes| Serves: 4

1-pound chicken breasts, skinless, boneless and cut into 4 slices
4 ounces goat cheese, crumbled
4 ounces ham, chopped
1 egg

¼ cup all-purpose flour
¼ cup parmesan cheese, grated
½ teaspoon onion powder
½ teaspoon garlic powder

1. Pound the chicken breasts with a mallet. 2. Stuff each piece of chicken with cheese and ham. Roll them up and secure with toothpicks. 3. In a shallow bowl, mix the remaining ingredients until well combined. Dip the chicken rolls into the egg/flour mixture. 4. Place the stuffed chicken in the Air Fryer basket. Install the wire rack on Level 3. Select the "AIR ROAST" function of Ninja Foodi Smart XL Pro Air Oven, set temperature to 400°F and time to 22 minutes. Select START/STOP to begin preheating. Cook the stuffed chicken breasts for about 22 minutes, turning them over halfway through the cooking time. Bon appétit!

Per Serving: Calories 486; Fat 32.3g; Sodium 589mg; Carbs 7.9g; Fiber 0.2g; Sugar 0.8g; Protein 39.3g

Spicy Chicken

Prep time: 10 minutes| Cook time: 15 minutes| Serves: 4

1-pound chicken breasts, boneless, skinless
½ cup rice wine
1 tablespoon stone-ground mustard
1 teaspoon garlic, minced

1 teaspoon black peppercorns, whole
1 teaspoon chili powder
¼ teaspoon sea salt

1. Install the wire rack on Level 3. Select the "AIR ROAST" function of Ninja Foodi Smart XL Pro Air Oven, set temperature to 380°F and time to 12 minutes. Select START/STOP to begin preheating. Place the chicken, wine, mustard, garlic, and whole peppercorns in a ceramic bowl. Cover and let it marinate for about 3 hours in your refrigerator. 2. Discard the marinade and place the chicken breasts in the Air Fryer basket. 3. Cook the chicken breasts for 12 minutes, turning them over halfway through the cooking time. 4. Season the chicken with the chili powder and salt. Serve immediately and enjoy!

Per Serving: Calories 206; Fat 11g; Sodium 421mg; Carbs 1g; Fiber 0.2g; Sugar 0.4g; Protein 24.2g

Chapter 4 Beef, pork, and lamb

Parmesan Pork Meatballs

Prep time: 15 minutes. | Cooking time: 10 minutes. | Servings: 4

12 ounces ground pork
2 ounces parmesan, grated
1 teaspoon Italian seasonings
1 teaspoon black pepper

1 teaspoon chili flakes
1 teaspoon fresh parsley, chopped
1 teaspoon avocado oil
1 teaspoon salt

1. Mix up ground pork, parmesan, Italian seasoning, black pepper, chili flakes, parsley, and salt. Make 4 balls from the mixture. 2. Select the Air Fry mode. Set the Ninja Foodi Smart XL Pro temperature to 365 degrees F/ 185 degrees C. Select Level "3" and set the time on your Ninja Foodi Smart XL Pro Air Fryer Oven to 10 minutes. Press Start/Pause to begin preheating. Continue to the next step when it is done preheating. 3. Then brush its air fryer basket with avocado oil. Put the pork balls inside. 4. Insert its air fryer basket into the level 3 of the oven and close the door. Cook them at 365 degrees F/ 185 degrees C for 10 minutes.

Per Serving: Calories 373; Fat 8.5 g; Sodium 4928 mg; Carbs 0.8g; Fiber 0.3g; Sugar 7.6g; Protein 74.5g

Boneless Ribeye Steaks

Prep time: 35 minutes. | Cooking time: 12 minutes. | Servings: 2–4

Boneless Ribeye
2 (8-ounces) boneless ribeye steaks
4 teaspoons Worcestershire sauce
½ teaspoon garlic powder

Pepper, to taste
4 teaspoons olive oil
Salt, to taste

1. Season steaks on both sides with Worcestershire sauce. Use the back of a spoon to spread. 2. Rub both sides of steaks with garlic powder and coarsely black pepper to taste. 3. Drizzle both sides of steaks with olive oil, again using the back of a spoon to spread evenly over surfaces. 4. Allow steaks to marinate for 30 minutes. 5. place both steaks in air fryer basket. Insert its air fryer basket into the level 3 of the oven and close the door. Cook on "Air Fry" Mode, select level 3, and set its temperature to 390 degrees F/ 200 degrees C for 5 minutes per side. Serve.

Per Serving: Calories 597; Fat 17.1 g; Sodium 723 mg; Carbs 66.5g; Fiber 9.3g; Sugar 45g; Protein 48.6g

Air Fried Calf's Liver

Prep time: 15 minutes. | Cooking time: 4–5 minutes. | Servings: 4

1 pound sliced calf's liver
Black pepper and salt
2 eggs
2 tablespoons milk
½ cup whole wheat flour

1½ cups panko breadcrumbs
½ cup plain breadcrumbs
½ teaspoon salt
¼ teaspoon pepper
Oil for misting or cooking spray

1. Cut liver slices crosswise into strips about ½-inch wide. Sprinkle with black pepper and salt to taste.2. Beat egg and milk in a shallow dish.3.Place wheat flour in a second shallow dish.4. In a third shallow dish, mix panko, plain breadcrumbs, ½ teaspoon salt, and ¼ teaspoon pepper.5. Preheat on "Air Fry" Mode, and set its temperature to 390 degrees F/ 200 degrees C. Select Level "3" and set the time on your Ninja Foodi Smart XL Pro Air Fryer Oven to 10 minutes. Press Start/Pause to begin preheating. Continue to the next step when it is done preheating.6. Dip liver strips in flour, egg wash, and then breadcrumbs, pressing in coating slightly to make crumbs stick.7. Cooking half the liver at a time, place strips in air fryer basket in a single layer, close but not touching.8. Cook on "Air Fry" Mode, select level 3, and set its temperature to 390 degrees F/ 200 degrees C for 4 to 5 minutes until done to your preference.9. Repeat step 7 to cook remaining liver.

Per Serving: Calories 379; Fat 20.9 g; Sodium 1598 mg; Carbs 10g; Fiber 2.2g; Sugar 2.1g; Protein 37g

Pork Stuffed Calzones

Prep time: 30 minutes. | Cooking time: 7–8 minutes. | Servings: 8

Filling
¼ pound ground pork sausage
½ teaspoon chile powder
¼ teaspoon ground cumin
⅛ teaspoon garlic powder
⅛ teaspoon onion powder
⅛ teaspoon oregano

Crust
2 cups white wheat flour
1 package (¼ ounce) rapid rise yeast
1 teaspoon salt
½ teaspoon chile powder

½ cup ricotta cheese
1-ounce sharp cheddar cheese, shredded
2 ounces pepper jack cheese, shredded
1 4-ounce can chopped green chiles, drained
Oil for misting or cooking spray
Salsa, sour cream, or guacamole

½ teaspoon ground cumin
1 cup warm water (125 degrees F/ 52 degrees C)
2 teaspoons olive oil

1. Crumble sausage into air fryer baking pan and stir in the filling seasonings: chile powder, cumin, garlic powder, onion powder, and oregano. Cook on "Air Fry" Mode, select level 3, and set its temperature to 390 degrees F/ 200 degrees C for 2 minutes. Stir, breaking apart, insert its air fryer basket in the level 3 and cook for 3 to 4 minutes, until well done.
2. To make dough, mix flour, yeast, salt, chile powder, and cumin. Stir in warm water and oil until soft dough forms. Turn out onto lightly floured board and knead for 3 or 4 minutes. Let dough rest for 10 minutes.3. Place the three cheeses in a medium bowl. Add cooked sausage and chiles and stir until well mixed. cut dough into 8 pieces.4. Working with 4 pieces of the prepared dough, press each into a circle about 5 inches in diameter. Top each dough circle with 2 heaping tablespoons of filling. Fold over into a half-moon shape and press edges together. Seal edges firmly to prevent leakage. Spray both sides with oil spray.5. Place 4 calzones in air fryer basket. Insert its air fryer basket into the level 3 of the oven and close the door. Cook on "Air Fry" Mode, select level 3, and set its temperature to 360 degrees F/ 180 degrees Cfor 5 minutes. Mist with oil or spray and cook for 2 to 3 minutes, until crust is done and nicely browned.6. While the first batch is cooking, press out the remaining dough, fill, and shape into calzones.7. Spray both sides with oil or cooking spray and cook for 5 minutes. If needed, mist with oil and continue cooking for 2 to 3 minutes longer. This second batch will cook a little faster than the first because your air fryer is already hot.8. Serve plain or with salsa, sour cream, or guacamole.
Per Serving: Calories 183; Fat 0.4 g; Sodium 4347 mg; Carbs 5.6g; Fiber 0.6g; Sugar 8.4g; Protein 40.2g

Lamb Stuffed Pita Pockets

Prep time: 15 minutes. | Cooking time: 5–7 minutes. | Servings: 4

Dressing
1 cup plain yogurt
1 tablespoon lemon juice
1 teaspoon dried dill weed, crushed
Meatballs
½ pound ground lamb
1 tablespoon diced onion
1 teaspoon dried parsley
1 teaspoon dried dill weed, crushed
¼ teaspoon oregano
Suggested toppings
Red onion, slivered
Seedless cucumber, thinly sliced
Crumbled feta cheese

1 teaspoon ground oregano
½ teaspoon salt

¼ teaspoon coriander
¼ teaspoon ground cumin
¼ teaspoon salt
4 pita halves

Sliced black olives
Chopped fresh peppers

1. Mix all the dressing ingredients and refrigerate while preparing lamb.2. Mix all meatball ingredients in a suitable bowl and stir to distribute seasonings.3. Shape meat mixture into 12 small meatballs, rounded or slightly flattened if you prefer.4. Cook on "Air Fry" Mode, select level 3, and set its temperature to 390 degrees F/ 200 degrees C degrees C for 5 to 7 minutes, until well done. Remove and drain on paper towels.5. To serve, pile meatballs in pita pockets and drizzle with dressing. Put the suggested toppings in pita pockets, if desired.
Per Serving: Calories 445; Fat 28.2 g; Sodium 322 mg; Carbs 6.2g; Fiber 2.2g; Sugar 1.4g; Protein 43.7g

Beef Steak

Prep time: 10 minutes. | Cooking time: 15 minutes. | Servings: 4

2 eggs
½ cup buttermilk
1½ cups flour
¾ teaspoon salt

½ teaspoon pepper
1-pound beef cube steaks
Black pepper and salt
Oil for misting or cooking spray

1. Beat eggs and buttermilk in a shallow dish.2. In another shallow dish, stir the flour, ½ teaspoon salt, and ¼ teaspoon pepper.3. Season cube steaks with remaining black pepper and salt to taste. Dip in flour, buttermilk egg wash, and then flour again.4. Spray both sides of steaks with oil or cooking spray.5. Cooking in 2 batches, place steaks in air fryer basket in single layer. Cook on "Air Fry" Mode, select level 3, and set its temperature to 360 degrees F/ 180 degrees Cfor 10 minutes. Spray tops of steaks with oil and cook 5 minutes until meat is well done.6. Repeat to cook remaining steaks.

Per Serving: Calories 512; Fat 7.1 g; Sodium 42 mg; Carbs 28.5g; Fiber 2.1g; Sugar 13.4g; Protein 1.2g

Italian Sausage with Peppers

Prep time: 10 minutes. | Cooking time: 21–25 minutes. | Servings: 6

1 6-ounce can tomato paste
⅔ cup water
1 8-ounce can tomato sauce
1 teaspoon dried parsley flakes
½ teaspoon garlic powder
⅛ teaspoon oregano
½ pound mild Italian bulk sausage

1 tablespoon extra-virgin olive oil
½ large onion, cut in 1-inch chunks
4 ounces fresh mushrooms, sliced
1 large green bell pepper, diced
8 ounces spaghetti, cooked
Parmesan cheese for serving

1. In a suitable saucepan or skillet, stir the tomato paste, water, tomato sauce, parsley, garlic, and oregano. Heat on stovetop over very low heat while preparing meat and vegetables.2. Break sausage into small chunks, about ½-inch pieces. Place in air fryer baking pan.3. Cook on "Air Fry" Mode, select level 3, and set its temperature to 390 degrees F/ 200 degrees C degrees C for 5 minutes. Stir. Cook 5 to 7 minutes longer until sausage is well done. Remove from pan, drain on paper towels, and add to the sauce mixture.4.If any sausage grease remains in baking pan, pour it off or use paper towels to soak it up.5. Place olive oil, onions, and mushrooms in pan and stir. Cook for 5 minutes or just until soft. Using a slotted spoon, transfer onions and mushrooms from baking pan into the sauce and sausage mixture.6. Place bell pepper chunks in air fryer baking pan and cook for 6 to 8 minutes until soft. When done, stir into sauce with sausage and other vegetables.7. Serve over cooked spaghetti with plenty of parmesan cheese.

Per Serving: Calories 210; Fat 5.4 g; Sodium 110 mg; Carbs 18.5g; Fiber 2.4g; Sugar 13.1g; Protein 23.5g

Kielbasa with Pineapple

Prep time: 15 minutes. | Cooking time: 10 minutes. | Servings: 2–4

Kielbasa chunks with pineapple & peppers
¾ pound kielbasa sausage
1 cup bell pepper chunks (any color)
1 8-ounce can pineapple chunks in juice, drained

1 tablespoon barbeque seasoning
1 tablespoon soy sauce
Cooking spray

1. Cut sausage into ½-inch slices.2. In a medium bowl, toss all the recipe ingredients together.3. Grease the Ninja Foody Smart Xl Pro's air fryer basket with nonstick cooking spray.4. Pour sausage mixture into the basket.5. Cook on "Air Fry" Mode, select level 3, and set its temperature to 390 degrees F/ 200 degrees C degrees C for approximately 5 minutes. Shake basket. Insert its air fryer basket into the level 3 of the oven and close the door. Cook an additional 5 minutes.

Per Serving: Calories 319; Fat 14.7 g; Sodium 92 mg; Carbs 30.3g; Fiber 4g; Sugar 12.3g; Protein 24g

Spiced Lamb Chops

Prep time: 30 minutes. | Cooking time: 20 minutes. | Servings: 2–3

Lamb chops
2 teaspoons oil
½ teaspoon ground rosemary
½ teaspoon lemon juice

1-pound lamb chops, approximately 1-inch thick
Black pepper and salt
Cooking spray

1. Mix the oil, rosemary, and lemon juice and rub into all sides of the lamb chops. Season to taste with black pepper and salt.2. Spray air fryer basket with nonstick spray and place lamb chops in it.3. Cook on "Air Fry" Mode, select level 3, and set its temperature to 360 degrees F/ 180 degrees Cfor 20 minutes. For rare chops, stop cooking after about 12 minutes and check for doneness.

Per Serving: Calories 362; Fat 22.6 g; Sodium 242 mg; Carbs 2.9g; Fiber 1.4g; Sugar 0.5g; Protein 37.4g

Sweet and Sour Meat Loaves

Prep time: 15 minutes. | Cooking time: 17–19 minutes. | Servings: 4

Sauce
¼ cup white vinegar
¼ cup brown sugar
Meat loaves
1 pound very lean ground beef
⅔ cup dry bread (approx. 1 slice torn into small pieces)
1 egg

2 tablespoons Worcestershire sauce
½ cup ketchup

⅓ cup minced onion
1 teaspoon salt
2 tablespoons ketchup

1. In a suitable saucepan, mix all sauce ingredients and bring to a boil. Remove from heat and stir to ensure that brown sugar dissolves completely.2. In a suitable bowl, mix the beef, bread, egg, onion, salt, and ketchup. Mix well.3. Divide the prepared meat mixture into 4 portions and shape each into a thick, round patty. Patties will be about 3 to 3½ inches in diameter, and all four should fit easily into its air fryer basket at once.4. Cook on "Air Fry" Mode, select level 3, and set its temperature to 360 degrees F/ 180 degrees C for 16 to 18 minutes, until meat is well done. Baste tops of mini loaves with a suitable amount of sauce, insert its air fryer basket in the level 3 and cook 1 minute.5. Serve hot with additional sauce on the side.

Per Serving: Calories 457; Fat 10.1 g; Sodium 423 mg; Carbs 1.6g; Fiber 0.5g; Sugar 0.4g; Protein 14.9g

Beef Crunch Wraps

Prep time: 5 minutes| Cook time: 2 minutes| Serves: 6

6 wheat tostadas
2 cups sour cream
2 cups Mexican blend cheese
2 cups shredded lettuce
12 ounces low-sodium nacho cheese

3 Roma tomatoes
6 12-inch wheat tortillas
11/3 cups water
2 packets low-sodium taco seasoning
2 pounds of lean ground beef

1. Select Level 3. Select the "AIR FRY" function of Ninja Foodi Smart XL Pro Air Oven, set temperature to 400°F and time to 2 minutes. Select START/STOP to begin preheating. 2. Make beef according to taco seasoning packets. Place 2/3 cup prepared beef, 4 tablespoons cheese, 1 tostada, 1/3 cup sour cream, 1/3 cup lettuce, 1/6th of tomatoes and 1/3 cup cheese on each tortilla. 3. Fold up the tortillas edges and repeat with the remaining ingredients. Lay the folded sides of tortillas down into the air fryer and spray with olive oil. Cook 2 minutes till browned.

Per Serving: Calories 311; Fat 6g; Sodium 112mg; Carbs 15g; Fiber 6g; Sugar 12g; Protein 2g

Meatball Subs with Marinara

Prep time: 15 minutes. | Cooking time: 9–11 minutes. | Servings: 4–8

Marinara sauce
1 15-ounce can diced tomatoes
1 teaspoon garlic powder
1 teaspoon dried basil
Meatballs
¼ pound ground turkey
¾ pound very lean ground beef
1 tablespoon milk
½ cup corn bread pieces
1 egg
¼ teaspoon salt
½ teaspoon dried onion
1 teaspoon garlic powder
Toppings, sliced or chopped:
Mushrooms
Jalapeño or banana peppers
Red or green bell pepper

½ teaspoon oregano
⅛ teaspoon salt
1 tablespoon robust olive oil

¼ teaspoon smoked paprika
¼ teaspoon crushed red pepper
1½ teaspoons dried parsley
¼ teaspoon oregano
2 teaspoons Worcestershire sauce
Sandwiches
4 large whole-grain sub or hoagie rolls, split

Red onions
Grated cheese

1. Place all marinara ingredients in saucepan and bring to a boil. Lower heat and simmer 10 minutes, uncovered.2. Mix all meatball the recipe ingredients in large bowl and stir. Mixture should be well blended but don't overwork it. Excessive mixing will toughen the meatballs.3. Divide meat into 16 equal portions and shape into balls.4. Cook on Air Fry mode and select level 3. Cook the balls at 360 degrees F/ 180 degrees Cuntil meat is done and juices run clear, about 9 to 11 minutes.5. While meatballs are cooking, taste marinara. If you prefer stronger flavors, then add more seasoning and simmer another 5 minutes.6. When meatballs finish cooking, drain them on paper towels.7. To assemble subs, place 4 meatballs on each sub roll, spoon sauce over meat, and add preferred toppings. Serve with additional marinara for dipping.

Per Serving: Calories 487; Fat 15 g; Sodium 4856 mg; Carbs 0g; Fiber 0g; Sugar 0g; Protein 85.4g

Meat Pies

Prep time: 20 minutes. | Cooking time: meat 10–12 minutes. | Servings: 8 pies

Filling
½ pound lean ground beef
¼ cup finely chopped onion
¼ cup finely chopped green bell pepper
⅛ teaspoon salt
Crust
2 cups self-rising flour
¼ cup butter, finely diced
1 cup milk
Egg wash

½ teaspoon garlic powder
½ teaspoon red pepper flakes
1 tablespoon low sodium Worcestershire sauce

1 egg
1 tablespoon water or milk
Oil for misting or cooking spray

1. Mix all filling ingredients well and shape into 4 small patties.2. Cook on Air Fry mode and Select Level "3". Cook patties in air fryer basket at 390 degrees F/ 200 degrees C for 10 to 12 minutes until well done.3. Place patties in large bowl and use fork and knife to crumble meat into very small pieces. Set aside.4. To make the crust, use a pastry blender or fork to cut the butter into the flour until well mixed. Add milk and stir until dough stiffens. 5. Divide dough into 8 equal portions. 6. On a floured surface, roll each portion of dough into a circle. The circle should be thin and about 5 inches in diameter, but don't worry about getting a perfect shape. Uneven circles result in a rustic look that many people prefer. 7. Spoon 2 tablespoons of meat filling onto each dough circle. 8. Brush egg wash all the way around the edge of dough circle, about ½-inch deep. (see tip.) 9. Fold each circle in half and press dough with tines of a dinner fork to seal the edges all the way around. 10. Brush tops of sealed meat pies with egg wash. 11. Cook filled pies in a single layer in air fryer basket at 360 degrees F/ 180 degrees Cfor 4 minutes. Spray tops with oil or cooking spray, turn pies over, and spray bottoms with oil or cooking spray. Cook for an additional 2 minutes. 12. Repeat previous step to cook remaining pies.

Per Serving: Calories 273; Fat 24 g; Sodium 1181 mg; Carbs 12.8g; Fiber 1g; Sugar 1.4g; Protein 20g

Pizza Tortilla Rolls

Prep time: 15 minutes. | Cooking time: 7–8 minutes. | Servings: 4

1 teaspoon butter
½ medium onion, slivered
½ red or green bell pepper, julienned
4 ounces fresh white mushrooms, chopped
8 flour tortillas (6- or 7-inch size)

½ cup pizza sauce
8 thin slices deli ham
24 pepperoni slices (about 1½ ounces)
1 cup shredded mozzarella cheese (about 4 ounces)
Oil for misting or cooking spray

1. Place butter, onions, bell pepper, and mushrooms in air fryer baking pan. Cook on "Air Fry" Mode, select level 3, and set its temperature to 390 degrees F/ 200 degrees for 3 minutes. Mix and cook 3 to 4 minutes longer until just crisp and soft. Remove pan and set aside.2. Spread roughly 2 teaspoons of pizza sauce on each tortilla half before assembling the rolls. Add three slices of pepperoni and a piece of ham on top. On top of the cheese, distribute the sautéed vegetables among the tortillas.3. Tortillas should be rolled, then oiled and, if necessary, fastened with toothpicks.4. Place 4 rolls in air fryer basket. Insert its air fryer basket into the level 3 of the oven and close the door. Cook for 4 minutes. Turn and cook 3 to 4 minutes, until heated through and lightly browned.5. Repeat step 4 to cook remaining pizza rolls.
Per Serving: Calories 559; Fat 23.8 g; Sodium 430 mg; Carbs 18.3g; Fiber 0.3g; Sugar 17.6g; Protein 65.8g

Beef and Cheese Egg Rolls

Prep time: 15 minutes| Cook time: 10 minutes| Serves: 3

6 egg roll wrappers
6 chopped dill pickle chips
1 tablespoon yellow mustard
3 tablespoons cream cheese
3 tablespoons shredded cheddar cheese

½ cup chopped onion
½ cup chopped bell pepper
¼ teaspoon onion powder
¼ teaspoon garlic powder
8 ounces of raw lean ground beef

1. Select Level 3. Select the "AIR FRY" function of Ninja Foodi Smart XL Pro Air Oven, set temperature to 392°F and time to 9 minutes. Select START/STOP to begin preheating. 2. In a skillet, add seasonings, beef, onion, and bell pepper. Stir and crumble beef till fully cooked and vegetables are soft. 3. Take skillet off the heat and add cream cheese, mustard, and cheddar cheese, stirring till melted. 4. Pour the beef mixture into a bowl and fold in pickles. Lay out egg wrappers and place 1/6th of beef mixture into each one. Moisten egg roll wrapper edges with water. Fold sides to the middle and seal them with water. Repeat with all other egg rolls. 5. Place rolls into the air fryer, one batch at a time. Cook for 7-9 minutes.
Per Serving: Calories 112; Fat 2g; Sodium 12mg; Carbs 8g; Fiber 1g; Sugar 6g; Protein 0g

Pepperoni Pizza Pockets

Prep time: 10 minutes. | Cooking time: 8–10 minutes. | Servings: 4

4 bread slices, 1-inch thick
Olive oil for misting
24 slices pepperoni (about 2 ounces)

1 ounce roasted red peppers, drained and patted dry
1-ounce pepper jack cheese cut into 4 slices
Pizza sauce

1. Spray both sides of bread slices with olive oil.2. Stand slices upright and cut a deep slit in the top to create a pocket—almost to the bottom crust but not all the way through.3. Stuff each bread pocket with 6 slices of pepperoni, a suitable strip of roasted red pepper, and a slice of cheese.4. Place bread pockets in air fryer basket, standing up. Cook on "Air Fry" Mode, select level 3, and set its temperature to 360 degrees F/ 180 degrees Cfor 8 to 10 minutes, until filling is heated through and bread is lightly browned. Serve while hot as is or with pizza sauce for dipping.
Per Serving: Calories 596; Fat 10.8 g; Sodium 7429 mg; Carbs 14.9g; Fiber 1.9g; Sugar 21.9g; Protein 112.2g

Sirloin Steak with Sausage gravy

Prep time: 10 minutes| Cook time: 15 minutes| Serves: 2

1 teaspoon pepper
2 cups almond milk
2 tablespoons almond flour
6 ounces ground sausage meat
1 teaspoon pepper
1 teaspoon salt

1 teaspoon garlic powder
1 teaspoon onion powder
1 cup panko breadcrumbs
1 cup almond flour
3 beaten eggs
6 ounces sirloin steak, pounded till thin

1. Slide basket into rails of Level 3. Select the "AIR FRY" function of Ninja Foodi Smart XL Pro Air Oven, set temperature to 370°F and time to 12 minutes. Select START/STOP to begin preheating. 2. Season panko breadcrumbs with spices. Dredge steak in flour, then egg, and then seasoned panko mixture. Place into air fryer basket. Cook 12 minutes. 3. To make sausage gravy, cook sausage and drain off fat, but reserve 2 tablespoons. Add flour to sausage and mix until incorporated. Gradually mix in milk over medium to high heat till it becomes thick. Season mixture with pepper and cook 3 minutes longer. Serve steak topped with gravy and enjoy!
Per Serving: Calories 30; Fat 13g; Sodium 12mg; Carbs 49g; Fiber 4g; Sugar 6g; Protein 3g

Fried Beef Taco Egg Rolls

Prep time: 15 minutes| Cook time: 12 minutes| Serves: 4

1 teaspoon cilantro
2 chopped garlic cloves
1 tablespoon olive oil
1 cup shredded Mexican cheese
½ packet taco seasoning

½ can cilantro lime rotel
½ chopped onion
16 egg roll wrappers
1-pound lean ground beef

1. Select Level 3. Select the "AIR FRY" function of Ninja Foodi Smart XL Pro Air Oven, set temperature to 400°F and time to 12 minutes. Select START/STOP to begin preheating. 2. Add onions and garlic to a skillet, cooking till fragrant. Then add taco seasoning, pepper, salt, and beef, cooking till beef is broken up into tiny pieces and cooked thoroughly. Add Rotel and stir well. 3. Lay out egg wrappers and brush with water to soften a bit. Load wrappers with beef filling and add cheese to each. Fold diagonally to close and use water to secure edges. Brush filled egg wrappers with olive oil and add to the air fryer. Cook 8 minutes, flip, and cook another 4 minutes. Sprinkled with cilantro, serve.
Per Serving: Calories 1052; Fat 50g; Sodium 438mg; Carbs 7g; Fiber 0g; Sugar 7g; Protein 132g

Crispy Mongolian-style Beef

Prep time: 10 minutes| Cook time: 12 minutes| Serves: 6 to 10

Olive oil
½ cup almond flour
Sauce:
½ cup chopped green onion
1 teaspoon red chili flakes
1 teaspoon almond flour
½ cup brown sugar
1 teaspoon hoisin sauce
½ cup water

2 pounds beef tenderloin or beef chuck, sliced into strips

½ cup rice vinegar
½ cup low-sodium soy sauce
1 tablespoon chopped garlic
1 tablespoon finely chopped ginger
2 tablespoons olive oil

1. Install the wire rack on Level 3. Select the "AIR ROAST" function of Ninja Foodi Smart XL Pro Air Oven, set temperature to 300°F and time to 10 minutes. Select START/STOP to begin preheating. 2. Toss beef strips in almond flour, ensuring they are coated well. Add to air fryer and cook 10 minutes. Meanwhile, add all sauce ingredients to the pan and bring to a boil. Mix well. Add beef strips to the sauce and cook 2 minutes. Serve over cauliflower rice!
Per Serving: Calories 173; Fat 13.6g; Sodium 281mg; Carbs 3g; Fiber 1g; Sugar 1g; Protein 10g

Beef and Cabbage Egg Rolls with Brandy Mustard Sauce

Prep time: 5 minutes| Cook time: 20 minutes| Serves: 5

Olive oil
½ cup orange marmalade
5 slices of Swiss cheese
Brandy Mustard Sauce:
1/16th teaspoon pepper
2 tablespoons whole grain mustard
1 teaspoon dry mustard powder
1 cup heavy cream
½ cup chicken stock
¼ cup brandy

4 cups corned beef and cabbage
1 egg
10 egg roll wrappers

¾ cup dry white wine
¼ teaspoon curry powder
½ tablespoon cilantro
1 minced shallot
2 tablespoons ghee

1. For mustard sauce, Cook shallots in ghee until softened. Add brandy along with wine, boil on low heat. Cook until liquids reduce. Add stock and seasonings. Manage to Simmer 5 minutes. Low the heat and whisk in heavy cream. Cook on low flame till sauce thicken. Place it in the fridge. 2. Select the "AIR FRY" function of Ninja Foodi Smart XL Pro Air Oven, set temperature to 390°F and time to 10 minutes. Select START/STOP to begin preheating. 3. Whisk the egg and set to the side. Lay out an egg wrapper and brush the edges with egg wash. Place corned beef mix and cabbage into the center along with marmalade and Swiss cheese. Fold the bottom corner over filling. Fold gently and make sure the filling is completely sealed. 3. Place rolls into the air fryer basket. Slide basket into rails of Level 3. Grease rolls with olive oil. Cook 10 minutes, shaking halfway through cooking. Serve with Brandy Mustard sauce and devour!
Per Serving: Calories 134; Fat 9.8g; Sodium 394mg; Carbs 2g; Fiber 0g; Sugar 1g; Protein 9g

Delicious Corned Beef Egg Rolls

Prep time: 5 minutes| Cook time: 8 minutes| Serves: 2 to 3

Swiss cheese
Can of sauerkraut

Sliced deli corned beef
Egg roll wrappers

1. Slide basket into rails of Level 3. Select the "AIR FRY" function of Ninja Foodi Smart XL Pro Air Oven, set temperature to 400°F and time to 8 minutes. Select START/STOP to begin preheating. 2. Cut corned beef and Swiss cheese into thin slices. Drain sauerkraut and dry well. Take egg roll wrapper and moisten edges with water. Stack center with corned beef and cheese till you reach desired thickness. Top off with sauerkraut. Fold the corner over the edge of filling. Bring up sides and glue with water. 3. Add to air fryer basket and spritz with olive oil. Cook 4 minutes, then flip and cook another 4 minutes.
Per Serving: Calories 227; Fat 9.8g; Sodium 525mg; Carbs 7g; Fiber 2g; Sugar 4g; Protein 28g

Air Fried Wax Bean

Prep time: 10 minutes. | Cooking time: 10 minutes. | Servings 4

1-pound fresh wax beans, trimmed
2 teaspoons olive oil
½ teaspoon onion powder

1 teaspoon garlic powder
½ teaspoon cumin powder
Black pepper and salt, to taste

1. Toss the wax beans with the remaining recipe ingredients. 2.Cook on Air Fry mode, select level 3. Air fry the wax beans at 390 degrees F for about 6 minutes, tossing the basket halfway through the Cooking time.3. Enjoy!
Per Serving: Calories 76; Fat 4.2 g; Sodium 135 mg; Carbs 2.4g; Fiber 0.5g; Sugar 0.3g; Protein 6.2g

Spicy Herbed Roast Beef

Prep time: 15 minutes| Cook time: 30 minutes| Serves: 5 to 6

½ teaspoon fresh rosemary
1 teaspoon dried thyme
¼ teaspoon pepper

1 teaspoon salt
4-pound top round roast beef
2 teaspoons olive oil

1. Install the wire rack on Level 3. Select the "AIR ROAST" function of Ninja Foodi Smart XL Pro Air Oven, set temperature to 360°F and time to 20 minutes. Select START/STOP to begin preheating. 2. Rub olive oil all over beef. Mix rosemary, thyme, pepper, and salt together and proceed to rub all sides of beef with spice mixture. Place seasoned beef into air fryer and cook 20 minutes. Allow it to rest for at least 10 minutes before slicing to serve.
Per Serving: Calories 248; Fat 21.1g; Sodium 429mg; Carbs 2g; Fiber 0g; Sugar 1g; Protein 12g

Tasty Steak and Broccoli

Prep time: 10 minutes| Cook time: 15 minutes| Serves: 4

1 minced garlic clove
1 sliced ginger root
1 tablespoon olive oil
1 teaspoon almond flour
1 teaspoon sweetener of choice
1 teaspoon low-sodium soy sauce

1/3 cup sherry
2 teaspoons sesame oil
1/3 cup oyster sauce
1 pounds of broccoli
¾ pound round steak

1. Select Level 3. Select the "AIR FRY" function of Ninja Foodi Smart XL Pro Air Oven, set temperature to 400°F and time to 12 minutes. Select START/STOP to begin preheating. Remove stems from broccoli and slice into florets. Slice steak into thin strips. Combine sweetener, soy sauce, sherry, almond flour, sesame oil, and oyster sauce together, stirring till sweetener dissolves. 2. Put strips of steak into the mixture and allow to marinate for 45 minutes to 2 hours. 3. Add broccoli and marinated steak to air fryer. Place garlic, ginger, and olive oil on top. Cook 12 minutes. Serve with cauliflower rice!
Per Serving: Calories 288; Fat 23.3g; Sodium 308mg; Carbs 6g; Fiber 1g; Sugar 5g; Protein 14g

Sweet Honey Mesquite Pork Chops

Prep time: 5 minutes| Cook time: 10 minutes| Serves: 2

2 tablespoons mesquite seasoning
¼ cup honey
1 tablespoon olive oil

1 tablespoon water
freshly ground black pepper
2 bone-in center pork chops

1. In a shallow glass dish, whisk the mesquite seasoning, honey, olive oil, water and black pepper together. Pierce the chops all over and on both sides with a fork or meat tenderizer. Add the pork chops to the marinade and massage the marinade into the chops. Cover and marinate for 30 minutes. 2. Select Level 3. Select the "AIR FRY" function of Ninja Foodi Smart XL Pro Air Oven, set temperature to 400°F and time to 6 minutes. Select START/STOP to begin preheating. 3. Transfer the pork chops to the air fryer basket and pour half of the marinade over the chops, reserving the remaining marinade. Air-fry the pork chops for 6 minutes. Flip and pour the marinade on top. Air-fry for an additional 3 minutes at 330°F. Then, increase the air fryer temperature to 400°F and air-fry the pork chops for an additional minute. 4. Let them rest for 5 minutes before serving. If you'd like a sauce for these chops, pour the cooked marinade from the bottom of the air fryer over the top.
Per Serving: Calories 69; Fat 7.2g; Sodium 486mg; Carbs 2g; Fiber 1g; Sugar 0g; Protein 0g

Roasted Beef Stuffed Peppers

Prep time: 5 minutes| Cook time: 25 minutes| Serves: 4

4 ounces shredded cheddar cheese
½ teaspoon pepper
½ teaspoon salt
1 teaspoon Worcestershire sauce
½ cup tomato sauce

8 ounces lean ground beef
1 teaspoon olive oil
1 minced garlic clove
½ chopped onion
2 green peppers

1. Select Level 3. Select the "AIR FRY" function of Ninja Foodi Smart XL Pro Air Oven, set temperature to 390°F and time to 20 minutes. Select START/STOP to begin preheating. 2. Spray with olive oil. Cut stems off bell peppers and remove seeds. Cook in boiling salted water for 3 minutes. Sauté garlic and onion together in a skillet until golden in color. Take skillet off the heat. Mix pepper, salt, Worcestershire sauce, ¼ cup of tomato sauce, half of cheese and beef together. 3. Divide meat mixture into pepper halves. Top filled peppers with remaining cheese and tomato sauce. Place filled peppers in air fryer and bake 15-20 minutes.

Per Serving: Calories 509; Fat 40.6g; Sodium 525mg; Carbs 8g; Fiber 2g; Sugar 5g; Protein 28g

Regular Beef Empanadas

Prep time: 15 minutes| Cook time: 10 minutes| Serves: 4

1 teaspoon water
1 egg white

1 cup picadillo
8 Goya empanada discs (thawed)

1. Select Level 3. Select the "AIR FRY" function of Ninja Foodi Smart XL Pro Air Oven, set temperature to 325°F and time to 8 minutes. Select START/STOP to begin preheating. 2. Spray basket with olive oil. Place 2 tablespoons of picadillo into the center of each disc. Fold disc in half and use a fork to seal edges. Repeat with all ingredients. 3. Whisk egg white with water and brush tops of empanadas with egg wash. Add 2-3 empanadas to the air fryer, cooking 8 minutes until golden. Repeat till you cook all the filled empanadas.

Per Serving: Calories 200; Fat 15.6g; Sodium 165mg; Carbs 5g; Fiber 1g; Sugar 2g; Protein 10g

Hoisin Glazed Pork Chops

Prep time: 5 minutes| Cook time: 12 minutes| Serves: 2 to 3

3 tablespoons hoisin sauce
¼ cup honey
1 tablespoon soy sauce
3 tablespoons rice vinegar
2 tablespoons brown sugar

1½ teaspoons grated fresh ginger
2 teaspoons Sriracha sauce
2 to 3 bone-in center cut pork chops, 1-inch thick (about 1¼ pounds)
chopped scallions, for garnish

1. Combine the hoisin sauce, honey, soy sauce, rice vinegar, brown sugar, ginger, and Sriracha sauce in a small saucepan. Whisk the ingredients and boil over medium-high heat on the stovetop. Lower the heat and manage to simmer the sauce until it has reduced in volume and thickened slightly – about 10 minutes. 2. Select Level 3. Select the "AIR FRY" function of Ninja Foodi Smart XL Pro Air Oven, set temperature to 400°F and time to 5 minutes. Select START/STOP to begin preheating. 3. Place the pork chops into the air fryer basket and pour half the hoisin BBQ sauce over the top. Air-fry for 6 minutes. Then, flip the chops over, pour the remaining hoisin BBQ sauce on top and air-fry for 5 to 6 more minutes, depending on the thickness of the pork chops. The internal temperature of the pork chops should be 155°F when tested with an instant-read thermometer. 4. You can spoon a little of the sauce from the bottom drawer of the air fryer over the top if desired. Sprinkle with chopped scallions and serve.

Per Serving: Calories 293; Fat 13.8g; Sodium 855mg; Carbs 28g; Fiber 8g; Sugar 11g; Protein 19g

Cheesy Bacon and Pear Stuffed Pork Chops

Prep time: 5 minutes| Cook time: 6 to 18 minutes| Serves: 3

4 slices bacon, chopped
1 tablespoon butter
½ cup finely diced onion
⅓ cup chicken stock
1½ cups seasoned stuffing cubes
1 egg, beaten
½ teaspoon dried thyme

½ teaspoon salt
⅛ teaspoon black pepper
1 pear, finely diced
⅓ cup crumbled blue cheese
3 boneless center-cut pork chops (2-inch thick)
olive oil
salt and freshly ground black pepper

1. Select Level 3. Select the "AIR FRY" function of Ninja Foodi Smart XL Pro Air Oven, set temperature to 400°F and time to 6 minutes. Select START/STOP to begin preheating. 2. Place the bacon into the air fryer basket and air-fry for 6 minutes, stirring halfway through the cooking time. Pour out the grease from the bottom of the air fryer. 3. To make the stuffing, melt the butter in a medium saucepan over medium heat on the stovetop. Cook the onion for a few minutes, until it starts to soften. Add the chicken stock and simmer for 1 minute. Add the stuffing cubes. Stir until the stock has been absorbed. Add the bacon, egg, dried thyme, salt and freshly ground black pepper, and stir until combined. Fold in the diced pear and crumbled blue cheese. 4. Place the chops on a cutting board. Using the palm of your hand to hold the chop flat and steady, slice into the side of the pork chop to make a pocket in the center of the chop. Leave about an inch of chop uncut and make sure you don't cut all the way through the pork chop. Brush chops with olive oil and season with salt and freshly ground black pepper. Stuff each pork chop with a third of the stuffing, packing the stuffing tightly inside the pocket. 5. Preheat the air fryer to 360°F. Spray or brush the sides of the air fryer basket with oil. Place the chops in the air fryer basket with the open stuffed edge of the pork chop facing the outside edges of the basket. 6. Air-fry the pork chops for 18 minutes, turning the pork chops over halfway through the cooking time. Let rest and then transfer to a serving platter.
Per Serving: Calories 151; Fat 7.5g; Sodium 621mg; Carbs 20g; Fiber 5g; Sugar 2g; Protein 5g

Herbed Beef Roast with Onion

Prep time: 15 minutes| Cook time: 45 minutes| Serves: 4

1½ pounds beef eye round roast
1 tablespoon olive oil
Sea salt
Ground black pepper, to taste

1 onion, sliced
1 rosemary sprig
1 thyme sprig

1. Select Level 3. Select the "AIR FRY" function of Ninja Foodi Smart XL Pro Air Oven, set temperature to 390°F and time to 45 minutes. Select START/STOP to begin preheating. 2. Toss the beef with the olive oil, salt, and black pepper; place the beef in the Air Fryer basket. Cook the beef eye round roast for 45 minutes, turning it over halfway through the cooking time. Top the beef with the onion, rosemary, and thyme. Continue to cook an additional 10 minutes. Enjoy!
Per Serving: Calories 268; Fat 13.6g; Sodium 348mg; Carbs 1.2g; Fiber 0.2g; Sugar 0.6g; Protein 35.2g

Herbed Porterhouse Steak

Prep time: 5 minutes| Cook time: 15 minutes| Serves: 4

1½ pounds Porterhouse steak
1 tablespoon olive oil
Kosher salt
Ground black pepper
½ teaspoon cayenne pepper

1 teaspoon dried parsley
1 teaspoon dried oregano
½ teaspoon dried basil
2 tablespoons butter
2 garlic cloves, minced

1. Select Level 3. Select the "ROAST" function of Ninja Foodi Smart XL Pro Air Oven, set temperature to 400°F and time to 12 minutes. Select START/STOP to begin preheating. Toss the steak with the remaining ingredients; place the steak in the Air Fryer basket. Cook the steak for 12 minutes, turning it over halfway through the cooking time. Bon appétit!
Per Serving: Calories 326; Fat 19.6g; Sodium 458mg; Carbs 1.9g; Fiber 0.4g; Sugar 0.6g; Protein 35.6g

Pistachio Crusted Rack of Lamb

Prep time: 5 minutes| Cook time: 19 minutes| Serves: 2

½ cup finely chopped pistachios
3 tablespoons panko breadcrumbs
1 teaspoon chopped fresh rosemary
2 teaspoons chopped fresh oregano

salt and freshly ground black pepper
1 tablespoon olive oil
1 rack of lamb, bones trimmed of fat
1 tablespoon Dijon mustard

1. Select Level 3. Select the "AIR FRY" function of Ninja Foodi Smart XL Pro Air Oven, set temperature to 380°F and time to 12 minutes. Select START/STOP to begin preheating. 2. Combine the pistachios, breadcrumbs, rosemary, oregano, salt and pepper in a small bowl. Grease in the oil and stir to combine. 3. Season the rack of lamb with salt and pepper on all sides and transfer it to the air fryer basket with the fat side facing up. Air-fry the lamb for 12 minutes. Remove the lamb and brush the fat side of the lamb rack with the Dijon mustard. Coat the rack with pistachio mixture, pressing the breadcrumbs onto the lamb with your hands and rolling the bottom of the rack in any of the crumbs that fall off. 4. Return the rack of lamb to the air fryer and air-fry for another 3 to 7 minutes. Add or subtract a couple of minutes for lamb that is more or less well cooked. 5.Let the lamb rest for at least 5 minutes. Then, slice into chops and serve.
Per Serving: Calories 56; Fat 2.2g; Sodium 177mg; Carbs 5g; Fiber 1g; Sugar 1g; Protein 5g

Cheese Lamb Hamburgers

Prep time: 5 minutes| Cook time: 15 minutes| Serves: 3 to 4

2 teaspoons olive oil
⅓ onion, finely chopped
1 clove garlic, minced
1-pound ground lamb
2 tablespoons fresh parsley, finely chopped
1½ teaspoons fresh oregano, finely chopped

½ cup black olives, finely chopped
⅓ cup crumbled feta cheese
½ teaspoon salt
freshly ground black pepper
4 thick pita breads
toppings and condiments

1. Pre-heat a skillet on the stovetop. Cook the onion in olive oil until tender, but not browned. Add in the garlic and cook. Place the cooked onion and garlic to a bowl and add the lamb, parsley along with oregano, olives, cheese, salt and pepper. Mix the ingredients .2. Divide the mix into 4 portions and form the hamburgers. 3. Select Level 3. Select the "AIR FRY" function of Ninja Foodi Smart XL Pro Air Oven, set temperature to 370°F and time to 5 minutes. Select START/STOP to begin preheating. 4. Air-fry the burgers for 5 minutes. Flip the burgers over and air-fry for another 8 minutes. Cook the breads in the air fryer for 2 minutes. Place the burgers into the toasted breads, and serve with a tzatziki sauce or some mayonnaise.
Per Serving: Calories 74; Fat 1.9g; Sodium 685mg; Carbs 9g; Fiber 7g; Sugar 2g; Protein 9g

Herbed Tenderloin with Fried Apples

Prep time: 5 minutes| Cook time: 23 minutes| Serves: 2 to 3

1 pork tenderloin (about 1-pound)
2 tablespoons coarse brown mustard
salt and freshly ground black pepper
1½ teaspoons finely chopped fresh rosemary, plus sprigs for

garnish
2 apples, cored and cut into 8 wedges
1 tablespoon butter, melted
1 teaspoon brown sugar

1. Select Level 3. Select the "AIR FRY" function of Ninja Foodi Smart XL Pro Air Oven, set temperature to 370°F and time to 10 minutes. Select START/STOP to begin preheating. 2. Cut the pork tenderloin in half so that you have two pieces that fit into the air fryer basket. Brush the mustard onto both halves of the pork tenderloin and then season with salt, pepper and the rosemary. Place the pork tenderloin halves into the air fryer basket and cook for 10 minutes. Turn the pork over and air-fry for an additional 5 to 8 minutes. If your pork tenderloin is especially thick, you may need to add a minute or two, but it's better to check the pork and add time, than to overcook it. 3. Let the pork rest for 5 minutes. In the meantime, toss the apple wedges with the butter and brown sugar and air-fry at 400°F for 8 minutes, shaking the basket once or twice during the cooking process so the apples cook and brown evenly. 4. Slice the pork on the bias. Serve with the fried apples scattered over the top and a few sprigs of rosemary as garnish.
Per Serving: Calories 25; Fat 0.1g; Sodium 546mg; Carbs 3g; Fiber 1g; Sugar 0g; Protein 3g

Lamb Koftas with Cucumber-Yogurt Dip

Prep time: 5 minutes| Cook time: 8 minutes| Serves: 3 to 4

For the lamb:
1-pound ground lamb
1 teaspoon ground cumin
1 teaspoon ground coriander
2 tablespoons chopped fresh mint
For the cucumber-yogurt dip:
½ English cucumber, grated (1 cup)
salt
½ clove garlic, finely minced
1 cup plain yogurt

1 egg, beaten
½ teaspoon salt
freshly ground black pepper

1 tablespoon olive oil
1 tablespoon chopped fresh dill
freshly ground black pepper

1. For the lamb: Combine ingredients and mix well. Divide the mixture into 10 portions. Make ball from portions and then by cupping the meatball in your hand, shape it into an oval. 2. Select Level 3. Select the "AIR FRY" function of Ninja Foodi Smart XL Pro Air Oven, set temperature to 400°F and time to 8 minutes. Select START/STOP to begin preheating. 3. Air-fry the koftas for 8 minutes. 4. For the cucumber-yogurt dip: Place the grated cucumber in a strainer and sprinkle with salt. Let this drain while the koftas are cooking. 2. Meanwhile, combine the garlic, yogurt, oil and fresh dill in a bowl. Just before serving, stir the cucumber into the yogurt sauce and season to taste with freshly ground black pepper. 5. Serve warm with the cucumber-yogurt dip.
Per Serving: Calories 217; Fat 21.8g; Sodium 207mg; Carbs 7g; Fiber 4g; Sugar 3g; Protein 2g

Easy Roast Beef

Prep time: 10 minutes| Cook time: 45 minutes| Serves: 6 to 8

Roast beef
1 tablespoon olive oil

Seasonings of choice

1. Install the wire rack on Level 3. Select the "AIR ROAST" function of Ninja Foodi Smart XL Pro Air Oven, set temperature to 390°F and time to 30 minutes. Select START/STOP to begin preheating. 2. Place roast in a bowl and toss with olive oil and desired seasonings. Put seasoned roast into the air fryer and cook for 30 minutes. Flip roast when the timer sounds and cook another 15 minutes.
Per Serving: Calories 429; Fat 32.4g; Sodium 325mg; Carbs 5g; Fiber 1g; Sugar 3g; Protein 28g

Simple Beef Patties

Prep time: 10 minutes| Cook time: 10 minutes| Serves: 4

1-pound lean ground beef
1 teaspoon dried parsley
½ teaspoon dried oregano
½ teaspoon pepper
½ teaspoon salt

½ teaspoon onion powder
½ teaspoon garlic powder
Few drops of liquid smoke
1 teaspoon Worcestershire sauce

1. Select Level 3. Select the "AIR FRY" function of Ninja Foodi Smart XL Pro Air Oven, set temperature to 350°F and time to 10 minutes. Select START/STOP to begin preheating. 2. Mix all seasonings together till combined. Place beef in a bowl and add seasonings. Mix well, but do not overmix. Make 4 patties from the mixture and, using your thumb, make an indent in the center of each patty. Add patties to air fryer basket and cook 10 minutes. No need to turn!
Per Serving: Calories 76; Fat 5.7g; Sodium 63mg; Carbs 1g; Fiber 0g; Sugar 1g; Protein 5g

Chapter 5 Fish and seafood

Fried Shrimp

Prep time: 10 minutes. | Cooking time: 15 minutes. | Servings 4

1 ½ pounds shrimp, cleaned and deveined
½ cup all-purpose flour
½ teaspoon shallot powder
½ teaspoon garlic powder
1 teaspoon red pepper flakes, crushed

Black pepper and salt, to taste
2 large eggs
1 cup crackers, crushed
½ cup parmesan cheese, grated

1. In a suitable shallow bowl, mix the flour and spices. Beat the eggs in the second bowl, and mix the crackers and cheese in the third bowl. 2. Dip the shrimp in the flour mixture, then in the whisked eggs; finally, roll the shrimp over the cracker/cheese mixture until they are well coated on all sides. 3. Spread the shrimp in a well-greased air fryer cooking basket. 4. Cook the shrimp on Air Fry mode on level 3 at 400 degrees F/ 200 degrees C for about 15 minutes.5. Bon appétit!

Per Serving: Calories 399; Fat 13 g; Sodium 626 mg; Carbs 52.9g; Fiber 8.8g; Sugar 3.9g; Protein 19.6g

Swordfish Steaks

Prep time: 10 minutes. | Cooking time: 10 minutes. | Servings 4

1-pound swordfish steaks
2 tablespoons olive oil
2 tablespoons fresh mint leaves, chopped
3 tablespoons fresh lemon juice

1 teaspoon garlic powder
½ teaspoon shallot powder
Black pepper and salt, to taste

1. Toss the swordfish steaks with the remaining recipe ingredients and place them in a lightly oiled air fryer cooking basket. 2. Cook the swordfish steaks on Air Fry mode on level 3 at 400 degrees F/ 200 degrees C for about 10 minutes, turning them over halfway through the Cooking time. 3. Bon appétit!

Per Serving: Calories 213; Fat 4.1 g; Sodium 303 mg; Carbs 37.9g; Fiber 1.5g; Sugar 1.9g; Protein 26.6g

Tuna Croquettes

Prep time: 10 minutes| Cook time: 8 minutes| Serves: 2

2 (5-ounce) cans tuna, drained
1 (8-ounce) package cream cheese, softened
½ cup finely shredded cheddar cheese
2 tablespoons diced onions
For Serving:
Cherry tomatoes
Mayonnaise

2 teaspoons prepared yellow mustard
1 large egg
1½ cups pork dust
Fresh dill, for garnish

Prepared yellow mustard

1. Select Level 3. Select the "AIR FRY" function of Ninja Foodi Smart XL Pro Air Oven, set temperature to 400°F and time to 5 minutes. Select START/STOP to begin preheating. 2. Make the patties: In a large bowl, stir together the tuna, cream cheese, cheddar cheese, onions, mustard, and egg until well combined. 3. Place the pork dust in a shallow bowl. 4. Form the tuna mixture into twelve 1½-inch balls. Roll the balls in the pork dust and use your hands to press it into a thick crust around each ball. Flatten the balls into ½-inch-thick patties. 5. Working in batches to avoid overcrowding, place the patties in the air fryer basket, leaving space between them. Cook for 8 minutes, or until golden and crispy, flipping halfway through. 6. Garnish the croquettes with fresh dill, if desired, and serve with cherry tomatoes and dollops of mayo and mustard on the side.

Per Serving: Calories 354; Fat 7.9g; Sodium 704mg; Carbs 6g; Fiber 3.6g; Sugar 6g; Protein 18g

Air Fried Calamari

Prep time: 10 minutes. | Cooking time: 5 minutes. | Servings 4

1 pound calamari, sliced into rings
2 garlic cloves, minced
1 teaspoon red pepper flakes
2 tablespoons dry white wine
2 tablespoons olive oil

2 tablespoons fresh lemon juice
1 teaspoon basil, chopped
1 teaspoon dill, chopped
1 teaspoon parsley, chopped
Salt and black pepper, to taste

1. Toss all the recipe ingredients in a lightly greased air fryer cooking basket. 2. Cook your calamari on Air Fry mode on level 3 at 400 degrees F/ 200 degrees C for 5 minutes, tossing the basket halfway through the Cooking time. 3. Bon appétit!

Per Serving: Calories 249; Fat 5.7 g; Sodium 574 mg; Carbs 23.9g; Fiber 0.9g; Sugar 1.9g; Protein 3.6g

Mustard Calamari

Prep time: 10 minutes. | Cooking time: 5 minutes. | Servings 4

2 cups flour
Black pepper and salt, to taste
1 teaspoon garlic, minced

1 tablespoon mustard
2 tablespoons olive oil
1 pound calamari, sliced into rings

1. In a mixing bowl, thoroughly mix the flour, salt, black pepper, garlic, mustard, and, and olive oil. Mix to mix well.2. Now, dip your calamari into the flour mixture to coat. 3. Cook your calamari on Air Fry mode on level 3 at 400 degrees F/ 200 degrees C for 5 minutes, turning them over halfway through the Cooking time. 4. Bon appétit!

Per Serving: Calories 336; Fat 6g; Sodium 181mg; Carbs 1.3g; Fiber 0.2g; Sugar 0.4g; Protein 69.2g

Italian Squid with Cheese

Prep time: 10 minutes. | Cooking time: 10 minutes. | Servings 4

1 ½ pounds small squid tubes
2 tablespoons butter, melted
1 chili pepper, chopped
2 garlic cloves, minced
1 teaspoon red pepper flakes

Black pepper and salt, to taste
¼ cup dry white wine
2 tablespoons fresh lemon juice
1 teaspoon Mediterranean herb mix
2 tablespoons Parmigiano-Reggiano cheese, grated

1. Toss all the recipe ingredients, except for the Parmigiano-Reggiano cheese, in a lightly greased air fryer cooking basket. 2. Cook your squid on Air Fry mode on level 3 at 400 degrees F/ 200 degrees C for 5 minutes, tossing the basket halfway through the Cooking time. 3. Top the warm squid with the cheese. Bon appétit!

Per Serving: Calories 249; Fat 5.7 g; Sodium 574 mg; Carbs 23.9g; Fiber 0.9g; Sugar 1.9g; Protein 3.6g

Pollock Fishcakes

Prep time: 10 minutes. | Cooking time: 15 minutes. | Servings 4

1 pound pollock, chopped
1 teaspoon chili sauce
Black pepper and salt, to taste
4 tablespoons all-purpose

1 teaspoon smoked paprika
2 tablespoons olive oil
4 ciabatta buns

1. Mix all the recipe ingredients, except for the ciabatta buns, in a suitable bowl. Shape the prepared mixture into four patties and place them in a lightly oiled air fryer cooking basket. 2. Cook the fish patties on Air Fry mode on level 3 at 400 degrees F/ 200 degrees C for about 14 minutes, turning them over halfway through the Cooking time. 3. Serve on hamburger buns and enjoy!

Per Serving: Calories 416; Fat 8.3 g; Sodium 208 mg; Carbs 22.9g; Fiber 0.5g; Sugar 19g; Protein 60.6g

Air Fried Buttered Sea Bass

Prep time: 10 minutes. | Cooking time: 15 minutes. | Servings 3

2 tablespoons butter, room temperature
1-pound sea bass such
¼ cup dry white wine
¼ cup all-purpose flour

Black pepper and salt, to taste
1 teaspoon mustard seeds
1 teaspoon fennel seeds
2 cloves garlic, minced

1. Toss the fish with the remaining recipe ingredients; place them in a lightly oiled air fryer cooking basket. 2. Cook the fish on Air Fry mode on level 3 at 400 degrees F/ 200 degrees C for about 10 minutes, turning them over halfway through the Cooking time. 3. Bon appétit!

Per Serving: Calories 297; Fat 1g; Sodium 291mg; Carbs 35g; Fiber 1g; Sugar 9g; Protein 29g

Herbed Salmon Fillets

Prep time: 10 minutes. | Cooking time: 15 minutes. | Servings 4

1 ½ pounds salmon fillets
2 sprigs fresh rosemary
1 tablespoon fresh basil
1 tablespoon fresh thyme
1 tablespoon fresh dill

1 small lemon, juiced
2 tablespoons olive oil
Black pepper and salt, to taste
1 teaspoon stone-ground mustard
2 cloves garlic, chopped

1. Toss the salmon with the remaining recipe ingredients; place them in a lightly oiled air fryer cooking basket. 2. Cook the salmon fillets on Air Fry mode on level 3 at 380 degrees F/ 195 degrees C for about 12 minutes, turning them over halfway through the Cooking time. 3. Serve immediately and enjoy!

Per Serving: Calories 348; Fat 30g; Sodium 660mg; Carbs 5g; Fiber 0g; Sugar 0g; Protein 14g

Chili Calamari

Prep time: 10 minutes. | Cooking time: 10 minutes. | Servings 4

½ cup milk
1 cup all-purpose flour
2 tablespoons olive oil
1 teaspoon turmeric powder

Salt flakes and black, to taste
1 teaspoon paprika
1 red chili, minced
1 pound calamari, cut into rings

1. In a mixing bowl, thoroughly mix the milk, flour, olive oil, turmeric powder, salt, black pepper, paprika, and red chili. Mix to mix well.2. Now, dip your calamari into the flour mixture to coat. 3. Cook your calamari on Air Fry mode on level 3 at 400 degrees F/ 200 degrees C for 5 minutes, turning them over halfway through the Cooking time. Bon appétit!

Per Serving: Calories 257; Fat 10.4g; Sodium 431mg; Carbs 20g; Fiber 0g; Sugar 1.6g; Protein 21g

Italian Sea Bass

Prep time: 10 minutes. | Cooking time: 15 minutes. | Servings 4

1-pound sea bass
2 garlic cloves, minced
2 tablespoons olive oil

1 tablespoon Italian seasoning mix
Black pepper and salt, to taste
¼ cup dry white wine

1. Toss the fish with the remaining recipe ingredients; place them in a lightly oiled air fryer cooking basket.2. Cook the fish on Air Fry mode on level 3 at 400 degrees F/ 200 degrees C for about 15 minutes, turning them over halfway through the Cooking time. 3. Bon appétit!

Per Serving: Calories 305; Fat 15g; Sodium 482mg; Carbs 17g; Fiber 3g; Sugar 2g; Protein 35g

Shrimp Hoagie Rolls

Prep time: 10 minutes. | Cooking time: 10 minutes. | Servings 4

1-pound shrimp, peeled and chilled
1 teaspoon olive oil
1 stalks celery, sliced
1 English cucumber, sliced
1 shallot, sliced
1 tablespoon fresh dill, roughly chopped
1 tablespoon fresh parsley, roughly chopped

1 tablespoon fresh lime juice
1 tablespoon apple cider vinegar
½ cup mayonnaise
1 teaspoon creole seasoning mix
1 ½ teaspoons Dijon mustard
Salt and lemon pepper, to taste
4 hoagie rolls

1. Toss the shrimp and olive oil in the air fryer cooking basket. 2. Cook the shrimp on Air Fry mode on level 3 at 400 degrees F/ 200 degrees C for 6 minutes, tossing the basket halfway through the Cooking time. 3. Place the shrimp in a mixing bowl along with the remaining recipe ingredients; toss to mix and serve on the prepared hoagie rolls. 3. Bon appétit!
Per Serving: Calories 399; Fat 16g; Sodium 537mg; Carbs 28g; Fiber 3g; Sugar 10g; Protein 35g

Crispy Crab Patties with Sweet 'n' Sour Sauce

Prep time: 10 minutes| Cook time: 12 minutes| Serves: 8

Patties:
1 pound canned lump crabmeat, drained
1 (8-ounce) package cream cheese, softened
1 tablespoon chopped fresh chives
Coating:
1½ cups pork dust
Dipping Sauce:
½ cup chicken broth
⅓ cup coconut aminos or wheat-free tamari
⅓ cup Swerve sweetener
¼ cup tomato sauce
1 tablespoon coconut vinegar

1 large egg
1 teaspoon grated fresh ginger
1 clove garlic, minced

¼ teaspoon grated fresh ginger
1 clove garlic, smashed to a paste
Sliced green onions, for garnish
Fried Cauliflower Rice , for serving

1. Select Level 3. Select the "AIR FRY" function of Ninja Foodi Smart XL Pro Air Oven, set temperature to 400°F and time to 12 minutes. Select START/STOP to begin preheating. 2. In a medium-sized bowl, gently mix all the ingredients for the patties, without breaking up the crabmeat. 3. Form the crab mixture into 8 patties that are 2½ inches in diameter and ¾ inch thick. 4. Place the pork dust in a shallow dish. Place each patty in the pork dust. Use your hands to press the pork dust into the patties to form a crust. Place the patties in the air fryer, leaving space between them. Cook for 12 minutes, or until the crust is golden and crispy. 5. While the patties cook, make the dipping sauce: In a large saucepan, whisk together all the sauce ingredients. Simmer, then turn the heat down to medium until the sauce thickened, about 5 minutes. 6. Place the patties on a serving platter, drizzle with the dipping sauce, and garnish with sliced green onions, if desired. Serve the dipping sauce on the side. Serve with fried cauliflower rice, if desired.
Per Serving: Calories 354; Fat 7.9g; Sodium 704mg; Carbs 6g; Fiber 3.6g; Sugar 6g; Protein 18g

Bread Crusted Fish

Prep time: 5 minutes| Cook time: 12 minutes| Serves: 4

4 fish fillets
1 egg

5-ounces breadcrumbs
4 tablespoons olive oil

1. Select Level 3. Select the "AIR FRY" function of Ninja Foodi Smart XL Pro Air Oven, set temperature to 350°F and time to 12 minutes. Select START/STOP to begin preheating. 2. In a bowl, mix oil and breadcrumbs. Whisk egg. Gently dip the fish into egg and then into crumb mixture. Put into air fryer and cook for 12-minutes.
Per Serving: Calories 354; Fat 7.9g; Sodium 704mg; Carbs 6g; Fiber 3.6g; Sugar 6g; Protein 18g

Cheesy Fish Fingers

Prep time: 10 minutes. | Cooking time: 15 minutes. | Servings 4

½ cup all-purpose flour
Salt and black pepper
1 teaspoon cayenne pepper
½ teaspoon onion powder
1 tablespoon Italian parsley, chopped

1 teaspoon garlic powder
1 egg, whisked
½ cup pecorino Romano cheese, grated
1-pound monkfish, sliced into strips

1. In a shallow bowl, mix well the flour, spices, egg, and cheese. Dip the fish strips in the prepared batter until they are well coated on all sides.2. Spread the prepared fish strips in the air fryer cooking basket. 3. Cook the fish strips on Air Fry mode on level 3 at 400 degrees F/ 200 degrees C for about 10 minutes, shaking the basket halfway through the Cooking time.4. Bon appétit!

Per Serving: Calories 308; Fat 24g; Sodium 715mg; Carbs 0.8g; Fiber 0.1g; Sugar 0.1g; Protein 21.9g

Fish Croquettes

Prep time: 10 minutes. | Cooking time: 15 minutes. | Servings 4

1-pound catfish, skinless, boneless and chopped
2 tablespoons olive oil
2 cloves garlic, minced
1 small onion, minced

¼ cup all-purpose flour
Black pepper and salt, to taste
½ cup breadcrumbs

1. Mix all the recipe ingredients in a suitable bowl. Shape the prepared mixture into bite-sized balls and place them in a lightly oiled air fryer cooking basket. 2. Cook the fish croquettes on Air Fry mode on level 3 at 400 degrees F/ 200 degrees C for about 14 minutes, shaking the basket halfway through the Cooking time.3. Bon appétit!

Per Serving: Calories 275; Fat 1.4g; Sodium 582mg; Carbs 31.5g; Fiber 1.1g; Sugar 0.1g; Protein 29.8g

Calamari with Tangy Tomato Sauce

Prep time: 5 minutes| Cook time: 8 minutes| Serves: 4

3 lbs. calamari
1/3 cup olive oil
1 tablespoon fresh oregano
1 teaspoon lemon juice
Sauce:
1 lb. fresh whole tomatoes
3 cloves garlic, minced
1 stalk of celery, chopped
1 tablespoon olive oil

1 tablespoon garlic, minced
¼ teaspoon chopped fresh lemon peel
¼ teaspoon crushed red pepper
¼ cup vinegar

½ green bell pepper
Salt and pepper to taste
½ cup onion, chopped

1. Select Level 3. Select the "AIR FRY" function of Ninja Foodi Smart XL Pro Air Oven, set temperature to 390°F and time to 6 minutes. Select START/STOP to begin preheating. 2. To make the sauce, mix all the sauce ingredients and add to blender. Blend until mixture is smooth. Clean the calamari and slice it into ½-inch rings. 3. Season calamari with vinegar, red pepper, lemon peel, garlic, lemon juice, and oregano. Add oil to air fryer sheet pan. Add calamari with its juice. Air fry for about 6-minutes. Stir once and air fry for another 2-minutes. Serve with hot with sauce.

Per Serving: Calories 298; Fat 11g; Sodium 336mg; Carbs 10.2g; Fiber g; Sugar 6g; Protein 18g

Delicious Salmon & Eggs

Prep time: 5 minutes| Cook time: 10 minutes| Serves: 2

2 eggs
1 lb. salmon, seasoned and cooked
1 cup celery, chopped

1 onion, chopped
1 tablespoon olive oil
Salt and pepper to taste

1. Select Level 3. Select the "AIR FRY" function of Ninja Foodi Smart XL Pro Air Oven, set the temperature to 300°F and time to 10 minutes. Select START/STOP to begin preheating. 2. Whisk the eggs in a bowl. Add celery, onion, salt, and pepper. Add the oil to a round baking tray and pour in the egg mixture, then place in the air fryer. Let it cook for 10-minutes. When done, serve with cooked salmon.

Per Serving: Calories 354; Fat 7.9g; Sodium 704mg; Carbs 6g; Fiber 3.6g; Sugar 6g; Protein 18g

Air Fried Tilapia Fillets

Prep time: 5 minutes| Cook time: 15 minutes| Serves: 3

2 egg yolks
4 wheat buns
1 lb. tilapia fillets, sliced
1 tablespoon nectar

1 tablespoon hot sauce
3 teaspoons of sweet pickle relish
2 tablespoons mayonnaise
1 tablespoon fish sauce

1. Select Level 3. Select the "AIR FRY" function of Ninja Foodi Smart XL Pro Air Oven, set temperature to 300°F and time to 15 minutes. Select START/STOP to begin preheating. 2. Mix the fish sauce and egg yolks in a bowl. Add mayonnaise, sweet pickle relish, hot sauce, and nectar. 3. Pour mixture into round baking tray. Place tray inside air fryer with tilapia fillets inside. Cook for 15 minutes.

Per Serving: Calories 354; Fat 7.9g; Sodium 704mg; Carbs 6g; Fiber 3.6g; Sugar 6g; Protein 18g

Cod Meatballs

Prep time: 15 minutes. | Cooking time: 8 minutes. | Servings: 3

12 ounces cod fillet, grinded
1 teaspoon ground coriander
½ teaspoon ground cumin
½ teaspoon salt
1 teaspoon dried dill
½ teaspoon lemon zest, grated

½ teaspoon ground paprika
1 egg, beaten
1 teaspoon chives, chopped
½ teaspoon lemon juice
Cooking spray

1. In the bowl mix up grinded cod fillet, ground coriander, cumin, salt, dried dill, lemon zest, ground paprika, egg, chives, and lemon juice. Stir the prepared mixture with the help of the spoon until homogenous. 2. Select the Air Fry mode. Set the Ninja Foodi Smart XL Pro temperature to 400 degrees F/ 200 degrees C. Select Level "3" and set the time on your Ninja Foodi Smart XL Pro Air Fryer Oven to 8 minutes. Press Start/Pause to begin preheating. Continue to the next step when it is done preheating. 3. Grease its air fryer basket with cooking oil spray Make the medium size meatballs from the fish mixture and put them in the air fryer in one layer. 4. Insert its air fryer basket into the level 3 of the oven and close the door. Cook the cod cakes for 4 minutes. 5. Then flip them on another side and cook for 4 minutes more.

Per Serving: Calories 216; Fat 6.9 g; Sodium 31 mg; Carbs 38.5g; Fiber 5.6g; Sugar 6.7g; Protein 6.7g

Clam and Veggie balls

Prep time: 5 minutes| Cook time: 30 minutes| Serves: 4

2 cups clam meat
2 tablespoons olive oil
¾ cup water
1 cup chickpea flour

¼ teaspoon black pepper
½ cup shredded zucchini
1 cup shredded carrot

1. Select Level 3. Select the "AIR FRY" function of Ninja Foodi Smart XL Pro Air Oven, set temperature to 390°F and time to 30 minutes. Select START/STOP to begin preheating. 2. Mix clam meat, olive oil, shredded carrot and zucchini along with black pepper in a bowl. Form small balls using your hands. Mix chickpea flour and water to form batter. 3. Coat balls with batter. Place in air fryer and cook for 30-minutes.

Per Serving: Calories 354; Fat 7.9g; Sodium 704mg; Carbs 6g; Fiber 3.6g; Sugar 6g; Protein 18g

Crispy Nacho-Crusted Shrimp

Prep time: 5 minutes| Cook time: 8 minutes| Serves: 8

18 jumbo shrimps, peeled and deveined
1 egg, beaten

8-9-ounce nacho-flavored chips, crushed
Salt and pepper to taste

1. Prepare two shallow dishes, one with egg and one with crushed chips. Spice with salt and pepper. Dip shrimp in the egg and then coat in nacho crumbs. 2. Select Level 3. Select the "AIR FRY" function of Ninja Foodi Smart XL Pro Air Oven, set temperature to 350°F and time to 8 minutes. Select START/STOP to begin preheating. Arrange the shrimp in the air fryer and cook for 8-minutes.

Per Serving: Calories 354; Fat 7.9g; Sodium 704mg; Carbs 6g; Fiber 3.6g; Sugar 6g; Protein 18g

Tropical Shrimp with Spicy Mayo

Prep time: 10 minutes| Cook time: 6 minutes| Serves: 4

1-pound large shrimp (about 2 dozen), peeled and deveined, tails on
Fine sea salt and ground black pepper
2 large eggs
Spicy Mayo:
½ cup mayonnaise
2 tablespoons beef or chicken broth
For Serving: :
Microgreens

1 tablespoon water
½ cup unsweetened coconut flakes
½ cup pork dust

½ teaspoon hot sauce
½ teaspoon cayenne pepper

Thinly sliced radishes

1. Spray the air fryer basket with avocado oil. Select Level 3. Select the "AIR FRY" function of Ninja Foodi Smart XL Pro Air Oven, set temperature to 400°F and time to 6 minutes. Select START/STOP to begin preheating. 2. Season the shrimp well on all sides with salt and pepper. 3. Crack the eggs into a shallow baking dish, add the water and a pinch of salt and pepper, and whisk to combine. In baking dish, stir the coconut flakes and pork dust until well combined. 4. Dip one shrimp in the eggs and let any excess egg drip off, then dredge both sides of the shrimp in the coconut mixture. Spray the shrimp with avocado oil and place it in the air fryer basket. Repeat with the remaining shrimp, leaving space between them in the air fryer basket. 5. Cook the shrimp in the air fryer for 6 minutes, or until cooked through and no longer translucent, flipping halfway through. 6. While the shrimp cook, make the spicy mayo: In a medium-sized bowl, stir together all the spicy mayo ingredients until well combined. 7. Serve the shrimp on a bed of microgreens and thinly sliced radishes, if desired. Serve the spicy mayo on the side for dipping.

Per Serving: Calories 354; Fat 7.9g; Sodium 704mg; Carbs 6g; Fiber 3.6g; Sugar 6g; Protein 18g

Teriyaki Halibut Steak

Prep time: 5 minutes| Cook time: 12 minutes| Serves: 3

1 lb. halibut steak
2/3 cup soy sauce
¼ teaspoon ginger, ground
1 garlic clove, minced
¼ cup orange juice

¼ teaspoon crushed red pepper flakes
2 tablespoon lime juice
1 teaspoon liquid stevia
½ cup mirin

1. Prepare teriyaki glaze by combining all ingredients except halibut steak in a saucepan. Bring mixture to a boil, then reduce heat by half. Set aside and allow to cool. Pour half of the glaze into a re-sealable bag with halibut and place in the fridge for 30-minutes. 2. Select Level 3. Select the "AIR FRY" function of Ninja Foodi Smart XL Pro Air Oven, set temperature to 390°F and time to 12 minutes. Select START/STOP to begin preheating. Place marinated halibut in air fryer and cook for 12-minutes. When finished, brush some of the remaining glazes over halibut steak.
Per Serving: Calories 354; Fat 7.9g; Sodium 704mg; Carbs 6g; Fiber 3.6g; Sugar 6g; Protein 18g

Sweet and Spicy Tossed Calamari

Prep time: 5 minutes| Cook time: 13 minutes| Serves: 2

½ lb. calamari tubes, about ¼ inch wide, rinsed and patted dry
1 cup club soda
½ cup honey
Red pepper flakes to taste

1 cup almond flour
Salt and black pepper to taste
2 tablespoons sriracha

1. Select Level 3. Select the "AIR FRY" function of Ninja Foodi Smart XL Pro Air Oven, set temperature to 380°F and time to 11 minutes. Select START/STOP to begin preheating. 2. Cover calamari rings with club soda in a bowl. Set aside for 10-minutes. In another bowl, mix flour, salt, and black pepper. In a third bowl, combine honey, sriracha, and red pepper flakes. Drain the calamari, pat dry, and cover with flour mixture. 3. Grease your air fryer basket with cooking spray. Add calamari in one layer, leaving little space in between. Cook for 11-minutes. Shake basket a couple of times during the process. 4. Remove the calamari from the air fryer and cover with half of the honey sauce and place inside the air fryer again. Cook for an additional 2-minutes. When ready to serve, cover with remaining sauce.
Per Serving: Calories 354; Fat 7.9g; Sodium 704mg; Carbs 6g; Fiber 3.6g; Sugar 6g; Protein 18g

Tuna Stuffed Potatoes

Prep time: 5 minutes| Cook time: 30 minutes| Serves: 2

4 medium potatoes
1 teaspoon olive oil
½ tablespoon capers
Salt and pepper to taste
1 green onion, sliced

1 tablespoon Greek yogurt
½ teaspoon chili powder
½ can of tuna in oil, drained
2 boiled eggs, sliced

1. Install the wire rack on Level 3. Select the "AIR ROAST" function of Ninja Foodi Smart XL Pro Air Oven, set temperature to 355°F and time to 30 minutes. Select START/STOP to begin preheating. Soak the potatoes in water for 30-minutes. Pat dry with kitchen towel. 2. Brush the potatoes with olive oil. Place potatoes in air fryer and air fry for 30-minutes. 3. Put tuna in a bowl with yogurt and chili powder, mix well. Add half of the green onion plus salt and pepper. 4. Slit potatoes length-wise. Stuff tuna mixture in the middle of potatoes and place on a serving plate. Sprinkle with chili powder and remaining green onions over potatoes. 5. Serve with capers and a salad of your choice and topped with boiled egg slices.
Per Serving: Calories 354; Fat 7.9g; Sodium 704mg; Carbs 6g; Fiber 3.6g; Sugar 6g; Protein 18g

Kataifi Shrimp with Lemon Garlic Sauce

Prep time: 5 minutes| Cook time: 22 minutes| Serves: 5

20 large green shrimps,
peeled and deveined
7 tablespoons unsalted butter
12-ounces of kataifi pastry

Wedges of lemon or lime
Salt and pepper to taste
5 cloves of garlic, crushed
2 lemons, zested and juiced

1. In a pan, heat butter. Add the garlic and lemon zest, and sauté for about 2-minutes. Season with salt, pepper and lemon juice. Cover the shrimp with half of garlic butter sauce and set aside the remaining half of sauce. 2. Select Level 3. Select the "AIR FRY" function of Ninja Foodi Smart XL Pro Air Oven, set temperature to 360°F and time to 20 minutes. Select START/STOP to begin preheating. 3. Remove the pastry from the bag and tease out strands. On the countertop lay 6-inch strands. Roll shrimp and butter into pastry. Shrimp tail should be exposed. Repeat process for all shrimp. 4. Place the shrimp into air fryer for 10-minutes. Flip shrimp over and place back into air fryer for another 10-minutes. Serve with a salad and lime or lemon wedges. Dip the shrimp into the remaining garlic butter sauce.
Per Serving: Calories 354; Fat 7.9g; Sodium 704mg; Carbs 6g; Fiber 3.6g; Sugar 6g; Protein 18g

Delicious Fish Taco

Prep time: 5 minutes| Cook time: 8 minutes| Serves: 2

1½ cups almond flour
1 can of beer
1 teaspoon baking powder
1 teaspoon sea salt
½ cup salsa
8-ounces fresh halibut, sliced into small strips
Avocado Cream:
1 large avocado
¾ cup buttermilk

Corn tortillas
Cilantro, chopped
Cholula sauce to taste
2 tablespoons olive oil
2 chili peppers, sliced

½ lime juiced

1. Make your batter by mixing baking powder, 1 cup of flour, beer, and salt. Stir well. Cover the halibut with remaining ½ cup of flour and dip it into the batter to coat well. 2. Select Level 3. Select the "AIR FRY" function of Ninja Foodi Smart XL Pro Air oven, set temperature to 390°F and time to 8 minutes. Select START/STOP to begin preheating. 3. Grease air fry basket with olive oil. Cook the fish for 8-minutes. 3. Mix the avocado cream ingredients in a blender until smooth. Place the corn tortillas on a plate and cover with salsa. Set aside. 4. Put the fish on top of tortillas and cover with avocado cream. 5. Add Cholula sauce, sprinkle with cilantro and top with chili slices and serve.
Per Serving: Calories 354; Fat 7.9g; Sodium 704mg; Carbs 6g; Fiber 3.6g; Sugar 6g; Protein 18g

Crispy Salmon with Dill Sauce

Prep time: 5 minutes| Cook time: 23 minutes| Serves: 4

1½ lbs. of salmon
4 teaspoons olive oil
Dill Sauce:
½ cup non-fat Greek yogurt
½ cup light sour cream

Pinch of sea salt

2 tablespoons dill, finely chopped
Pinch of sea salt

1. Select Level 3. Select the "AIR FRY" function of Ninja Foodi Smart XL Pro Air Oven, set temperature to 270°F and time to 23 minutes. Select START/STOP to begin preheating. 2. Cut salmon into four 6-ounce portions and drizzle 1 teaspoon of olive oil over each piece. Season with sea salt. Place salmon into basket and cook for 23-minutes. 3. Make dill sauce. In a mixing bowl, mix sour cream, yogurt, chopped dill and sea salt. Top cooked salmon with sauce and garnish with additional dill and serve.
Per Serving: Calories 354; Fat 7.9g; Sodium 704mg; Carbs 6g; Fiber 3.6g; Sugar 6g; Protein 18g

Codfish and Oysters Teriyaki with Veggies

Prep time: 5 minutes| Cook time: 10 minutes| Serves: 2

1 tablespoon olive oil
6 pieces mini king oyster
mushrooms, thinly sliced
2 slices (1-inch) codfish
1 Napa cabbage leaf, sliced
Teriyaki Sauce:
1 teaspoon liquid stevia
2 tablespoons mirin

1 clove garlic, chopped
Salt to taste
1 green onion, minced
Veggies, steamed of your choice

2 tablespoons soy sauce

1. Make teriyaki sauce by mixing well all the ingredients then set aside. Grease the air fryer basket with oil. Place the mushrooms, garlic, Napa cabbage leaf, and salt inside. Layer the fish on top. 2. Select Level 3. Select the "AIR FRY" function of Ninja Foodi Smart XL Pro Air Oven, set temperature to 360°F and time to 5 minutes. Select START/STOP to begin preheating. 3. Place the basket in air fryer and cook for 5-minutes. Stir. Pour the teriyaki sauce over ingredients in the basket. Cook for an additional 5-minutes. Serve with your choice of steamed veggies.
Per Serving: Calories 354; Fat 7.9g; Sodium 704mg; Carbs 6g; Fiber 3.6g; Sugar 6g; Protein 18g

Grilled Barramundi with Tangy Butter Sauce

Prep time: 5 minutes| Cook time: 40 minutes| Serves: 2

1 lb. small potatoes
7-ounces barramundi fillets
1 teaspoon olive oil
Lemon Butter Sauce:
1 scallion, chopped
½ cup thickened cream
½ cup white wine
1 bay leaf
10 black peppercorns

¼ bunch of fresh thyme, chopped
Green beans, cooked, optional

1 clove garlic, chopped
8-ounces unsalted butter
1 lemon, juiced
Salt and pepper to taste

1. Select Level 3. Select the "AIR FRY" function of Ninja Foodi Smart XL Pro Air Oven, set temperature to 390°F and time to 20 minutes. Select START/STOP to begin preheating. 2. In a bowl, add potatoes, salt, thyme and olive oil. Mix ingredients well. Put potatoes into air fryer basket and cook for 20-minutes. Layer the fish fillets in a basket on top of potatoes. Cook for another 20-minutes. 3. In a skillet, heat scallion and garlic over medium-high heat and add the peppercorns and bay leaf. Pour the wine in and reduce heat to low. Add the thickened cream and stir to blend. Add the butter and whisk over low heat. When butter has melted, add salt, pepper, and lemon juice. Strain the sauce to remove peppercorns and bay leaf. 4. Place the fish and potatoes on a serving plate and add sauce and serve with green beans.
Per Serving: Calories 354; Fat 7.9g; Sodium 704mg; Carbs 6g; Fiber 3.6g; Sugar 6g; Protein 18g

Healthy Scallops

Prep time: 5 minutes| Cook time: 4 minutes| Serves: 2

12 medium sea scallops
1 teaspoon fine sea salt

¾ teaspoon ground black pepper
Fresh thyme leaves, for garnish

1. Spray the air fryer basket with avocado oil. Select Level 3. Select the "AIR FRY" function of Ninja Foodi Smart XL Pro Air Oven, set temperature to 390°F and time to 4 minutes. Select START/STOP to begin preheating. 2. Rinse the scallops and pat completely dry. Spray avocado oil on the scallops and season them with the salt and pepper. Place them in the air fryer basket, spacing them apart. Cook for 2 minutes, then flip the scallops and cook for another 2 minutes, or until cooked through and no longer translucent. Garnish with ground black pepper and thyme leaves, if desired.
Per Serving: Calories 354; Fat 7.9g; Sodium 704mg; Carbs 6g; Fiber 3.6g; Sugar 6g; Protein 18g

Garlic Butter Shrimp

Prep time: 5 minutes| Cook time: 8 minutes| Serves: 4

¼ cup unsalted butter
2 tablespoons fish stock or chicken broth
1 tablespoon lemon juice
2 cloves garlic, minced
2 tablespoons chopped fresh basil leaves

1 tablespoon parsley
1 teaspoon red pepper flakes
1-pound shrimp,
Fresh basil sprigs, for garnish

1. Select Level 3. Select the "AIR FRY" function of Ninja Foodi Smart XL Pro Air Oven, set temperature to 350°F and time to 5 minutes. Select START/STOP to begin preheating. 2. Place the butter, fish stock, lemon juice, garlic, basil, parsley, and red pepper flakes in a 6 by 3-inch pan, stir to combine, and place in the air fryer. Cook until fragrant and the garlic has softened. 3. Add the shrimp and stir to coat the shrimp in the sauce. Cook until the shrimp are pink, stirring after 3 minutes. Garnish with fresh basil sprigs and chopped parsley before serving.

Per Serving: Calories 354; Fat 7.9g; Sodium 704mg; Carbs 6g; Fiber 3.6g; Sugar 6g; Protein 18g

Tangy Cranberry Cod

Prep time: 5 minutes| Cook time: 20 minutes| Serves: 2

3 filets cod
1 tablespoon olive oil

3 tablespoons cranberry jam

1. Select Level 3. Select the "AIR FRY" function of Ninja Foodi Smart XL Pro Air Oven, set temperature to 390°F and time to 20 minutes. Select START/STOP to begin preheating. 2. Brush the cod filets with olive oil. Spoon a tablespoon of cranberry jam on each filet. Cook for 20-minutes.

Per Serving: Calories 354; Fat 7.9g; Sodium 704mg; Carbs 6g; Fiber 3.6g; Sugar 6g; Protein 18g

Chapter 6 Snack and appetizers

Sweet Chicken Wings

Prep time: 10 minutes. | Cooking time: 20 minutes. | Servings 5

2 pounds chicken wings
¼ cup agave syrup
2 tablespoons soy sauce
2 tablespoons scallions, chopped

2 tablespoons olive oil
1 teaspoon ginger, peeled and grated
2 cloves garlic, minced
Black pepper and salt, to taste

1. Toss the chicken wings with the remaining recipe ingredients. 2. Cook on Air Fry mode and select level 3. Cook the chicken wings at 380 degrees F/ 195 degrees C for 18 minutes, turning them over halfway through the Cooking time. Serve.
Per Serving: Calories 284; Fat 16g; Sodium 252mg; Carbs 31.6g; Fiber 0.9g; Sugar 6.6g; Protein 3.7g

Yam Chips

Prep time: 10 minutes. | Cooking time: 15 minutes. | Servings 2

1 large-sized yam, peeled and cut into ¼-inch sticks
1 tablespoon olive oil

Kosher salt and red pepper, to taste

1. Select the "Air Fry" Mode, press level 3, and set its temperature to 360 degrees F/ 180 degrees C and set the time to 15 minutes. Press Start/Pause to initiate preheating.2. Toss the yam with the remaining recipe ingredients and place them in the air fryer cooking basket. 3. Air fry the yam sticks for 15 minutes, tossing halfway through the Cooking time and working in batches. Enjoy!
Per Serving: Calories 149; Fat 1.2g; Sodium 3mg; Carbs 37.6g; Fiber 5.8g; Sugar 29g; Protein 1.1g

Potato Chips

Prep time: 10 minutes. | Cooking time: 16 minutes. | Servings 3

2 large-sized potatoes, peeled and thinly sliced
2 tablespoons olive oil
1 teaspoon Sichuan peppercorns

1 teaspoon garlic powder
½ teaspoon Chinese five-spice powder
Salt, to taste

1. Select the "Air Fry" Mode, press level 3, and set its temperature to 360 degrees F/ 180 degrees C Press Start/Pause to initiate preheating.2. Toss the potatoes with the remaining recipe ingredients and place them in the air fryer cooking basket. 3. Air fry the potato chips for 16 minutes, shaking the basket halfway through the Cooking time and working in batches.4. Enjoy!
Per Serving: Calories 127; Fat 14.2g; Sodium 672mg; Carbs 47.2g; Fiber 1.7g; Sugar 24.8g; Protein 4.4g

Tomato Chips with Cheese

Prep time: 10 minutes. | Cooking time: 20 minutes. | Servings 3

1 large-sized beefsteak tomatoes
2 tablespoons olive oil
½ teaspoon paprika
Salt, to taste

1 teaspoon garlic powder
1 tablespoon fresh cilantro, chopped
4 tablespoons pecorino cheese, grated

1. Toss the tomato slices with the olive oil and spices until they are well coated on all sides. 2. Spread the tomato slices in the air fryer cooking basket. 3. Cook on Air Fry mode and select level 3, cook the tomato slices at 360 degrees F/ 180 degrees Cfor about 10 minutes. Turn the temperature to 330 degrees F/ 165 degrees C and top the tomato slices with the cheese; now, continue to cook for 5 minutes. Bon appétit!
Per Serving: Calories 157; Fat 1.3g; Sodium 27mg; Carbs 1.3g; Fiber 1g; Sugar 2.2g; Protein 8.2g

Butter Sriracha Chicken Wings

Prep time: 10 minutes. | Cooking time: 18minutes. | Servings 4)

2 pounds chicken wings
1 tablespoon white vinegar
Black pepper and salt, to taste
1 teaspoon cayenne pepper

1 teaspoon garlic powder
½ teaspoon onion powder
4 tablespoons butter, room temperature
¼ cup sriracha sauce

1. Toss the chicken wings with the remaining recipe ingredients. 2. Cook on Air Fry mode and select level 3, cook the chicken wings at 380 degrees F/ 195 degrees C for 18 minutes, turning them over halfway through the Cooking time. Bon appétit!

Per Serving: Calories 192; Fat 9.3g; Sodium 133mg; Carbs 27.1g; Fiber 1.4g; Sugar 19g; Protein 3.2g

Eggplant Fries

Prep time: 10 minutes. | Cooking time: 15 minutes. | Servings 3

¾-pound eggplant
Black pepper and salt, to taste
½ teaspoon paprika

2 tablespoons olive oil
2 tablespoons balsamic vinegar

1. Toss the eggplant pieces with the remaining recipe ingredients until they are well coated on all sides. 2. Spread the eggplant in its air fryer basket. 3. Cook on Air Fry mode and select level 3, cook the eggplant at 400 degrees F/ 200 degrees C for about 15 minutes, shaking the basket halfway through the cooking time. Bon appétit!

Per Serving: Calories 204; Fat 9g; Sodium 91mg; Carbs 27g; Fiber 2.4g; Sugar 15g; Protein 1.3g

Crispy Ham 'n' Cheese Ravioli

Prep time: 15 minutes| Cook time: 10 minutes| Serves: 6

1 cup shredded cheddar cheese (about 4 ounces)
6 ounces cream cheese (¾ cup), softened
8 ounces thinly sliced ham (12 very large slices)
1 large egg

1 cup pork dust (see here)
Fresh parsley leaves, for garnish
Ranch Dressing (here), for serving

1. In a small bowl, stir together the cheddar cheese and cream cheese until well combined. 2. Assemble the ravioli: Lay one slice of ham on a sheet of parchment paper. Spoon about 2 heaping tablespoons of the filling into the center of the ham. Fold one end of the ham over the filling, making sure the ham completely covers the filling and meets the ham on the other side Fold the ends around the filling to make a square, making sure that the filling is covered well. Using your fingers, press down around the filling to even the ravioli out into a square shape. Repeat with the rest of the ham and filling; you should have 12 raviolis. 3. Crack the egg into a shallow bowl and beat well with a fork. Place the pork dust in another shallow bowl. 4. Gently dip each ravioli into the egg, then dredge it in the pork dust. Use your hands to press the pork dust into the ravioli, coating it well. Spray the ravioli with avocado oil and place it in the air fryer basket. Make sure to leave space between the ravioli. 5. Select Level 3. Select the "AIR FRY" function of Ninja Foodi Smart XL Pro Air Oven, set temperature to 400°F and time to 10 minutes. Select START/STOP to begin preheating. 6. Cook the ravioli in the air fryer for 10 minutes, or until crispy, flipping after 6 minutes. 7. Serve warm, garnished with fresh parsley and with ranch dressing for dipping if desired.8. Store leftovers in an airtight container in the fridge for up to 4 days.

Per Serving: Calories 354; Fat 7.9g; Sodium 704mg; Carbs 6g; Fiber 3.6g; Sugar 6g; Protein 18g

Spicy Nuts

Prep time: 10 minutes. | Cooking time: 6 minutes. | Servings 4

1 egg white lightly beaten
½ cup pecan halves
½ cup almonds
½ cup walnuts

Salt and cayenne pepper, to taste
1 teaspoon chili powder
½ teaspoon ground cinnamon
½ teaspoon ground allspice

1. Select the "Air Fry" Mode, press level 3. Set its temperature to 330 degrees F/ 165 degrees C. and set the time to 6 minutes. Press Start/Pause to initiate preheating.2. Mix the nuts with the rest of the recipe ingredients and place them in the air fryer cooking basket.3. Air fry the nuts for 6 minutes, shaking the basket halfway through the Cooking time and working in batches. Enjoy!

Per Serving: Calories 258; Fat 12.4g; Sodium 79mg; Carbs 34.3g; Fiber 1g; Sugar 17g; Protein 3.2g

Golden Beet Chips

Prep time: 10 minutes. | Cooking time: 35 minutes. | Servings 2

½ pound golden beets, peeled and thinly sliced
Kosher salt and black pepper, to taste
1 teaspoon paprika

2 tablespoons olive oil
½ teaspoon garlic powder
1 teaspoon ground turmeric

1. Select the "Air Fry" Mode, press level 3, set its temperature to 330 degrees F/ 165 degrees C and set the time to 30 minutes. Press Start/Pause to initiate preheating.2. Toss the beets with the remaining recipe ingredients and place them in the air fryer cooking basket. 3. Air fry your chips for 30 minutes, shaking the basket occasionally and working in batches.4. Enjoy!

Per Serving: Calories 175; Fat 13.1g; Sodium 154mg; Carbs 14g; Fiber 0.8g; Sugar 8.9g; Protein 0.7g

Cheese and Parsley Stuffed Mushrooms

Prep time: 10 minutes. | Cooking time: 10 minutes. | Servings 4

2 tablespoons olive oil
½ cup breadcrumbs
½ cup parmesan cheese, grated
1 teaspoon garlic, minced

1 tablespoon fresh parsley, chopped
1 tablespoon fresh chives, chopped
Black pepper and salt, to taste
1-pound button mushrooms, stems removed

1. In a mixing bowl, thoroughly mix the olive oil, breadcrumbs, parmesan cheese, garlic, parsley, chives, salt, and black pepper. 2. Divide the filling between your mushrooms. Spread the mushrooms in its air fryer basket. 3. Cook on Air Fry mode and select level 3, cook your mushrooms at 400 degrees F/ 200 degrees C for about 7 minutes, shaking the basket halfway through the Cooking time.Bon appétit!

Per Serving: Calories 273; Fat 24 g; Sodium 1181 mg; Carbs 12.8g; Fiber 1g; Sugar 1.4g; Protein 20g

Garlicky Kale Chips

Prep time: 10 minutes. | Cooking time: 10 minutes. | Servings 4

4 cups kale, torn into pieces
1 tablespoon sesame oil

1 teaspoon garlic powder
Black pepper and salt, to taste

1. Select the "Air Fry" Mode, press level 3, and set its temperature to 360 degrees F/ 180 degrees C Press Start/Pause to initiate preheating. 2. Toss the kale leaves with the remaining recipe ingredients and place them in the air fryer cooking basket. 3. Air fry your chips for 8 minutes, shaking the basket occasionally and working in batches.4. Enjoy!

Per Serving: Calories 157; Fat 10.1 g; Sodium 423 mg; Carbs 1.6g; Fiber 0.5g; Sugar 0.4g; Protein 14.9g

Bacon-Wrapped Sausages

Prep time: 10 minutes. | Cooking time: 20 minutes. | Servings 4

1-pound mini sausages
2 tablespoons tamari sauce
2 tablespoons maple syrup

1 teaspoon chili powder
Black pepper, to taste
4 ounces bacon, thinly slices

1. Toss the mini sausages with the tamari sauce, maple syrup, chili powder, and black pepper. 2. Wrap the mini sausages with the bacon. 3. Place the sausages in a lightly oiled air fryer cooking basket. 4. Select the "Air Fry" Mode, press level 3, cook the sausages at 380 degrees F/ 195 degrees C for 15 minutes, tossing the basket halfway through the Cooking time. 5. Serve warm and enjoy!

Per Serving: Calories 343; Fat 13.1 g; Sodium 1333 mg; Carbs 5.7g; Fiber 0.1g; Sugar 0.2g; Protein 43.6g

Hot Dog Roll

Prep time: 10 minutes. | Cooking time: 10 minutes. | Servings 6

6 ounces crescent rolls, refrigerated
1 tablespoon mustard

10 ounces mini hot dogs

1. Separate the prepared dough into triangles. Cut them lengthwise into 3 small triangles. Spread each triangle with mustard.2. Place a mini hot dog on the shortest side of each triangle and roll it up. 3. Place the rolls in the air fryer cooking basket. 4. Cook on Bake mode and select level 3, bake the rolls at 320 degrees F/ 160 degrees C for about 8 minutes, turning them over halfway through the Cooking time. Bon appétit!

Per Serving: Calories 199; Fat 17.9g; Sodium 525mg; Carbs 1.1g; Fiber 0.3g; Sugar 0.6g; Protein 9.9g

Ham 'n' Cheese Pies

Prep time: 10 minutes| Cook time: 12 minutes| Serves: 1

Dough:
1¾ cups shredded mozzarella cheese (about 7 ounces)
2 tablespoons unsalted butter
1 large egg
Filling:
8 thin slices ham
4 slices provolone or cheddar cheese

¾ cup blanched almond flour
⅛ teaspoon fine sea salt

¼ cup mayonnaise
Prepared yellow mustard, for serving

1. **Make the dough:** Place the mozzarella cheese and butter in a large bowl and microwave for 2 minutes, until the cheese is entirely melted. Stir well. Add in the egg and combine well. Add the almond flour and salt and combine well with the mixer. 2. Lay a piece of parchment paper on the countertop, spray it with avocado oil, and place the dough on it. Knead for about 3 minutes. The dough should be thick yet pliable. 3. Spray the air fryer basket with avocado oil. Select Level 3. Select the "AIR FRY" function of Ninja Foodi Smart XL Pro Air Oven, set temperature to 350°F and time to 10 minutes. Select START/STOP to begin preheating. 4. Separate the dough into 4 equal portions. Pat each portion out with your hands to form a small circle, about 4 inches in diameter. 5. Place 2 slices of ham and one slice of cheese in the center of each dough circle and smear a tablespoon of mayo on top. Seal each pie closed by folding the dough circle in half and crimping the edges with your fingers. 6. Transfer the pies to the air fryer basket, leaving space between them. Cook for 10 minutes, or until golden brown. Drizzle with mustard before serving, if desired. 7. Store leftovers in an airtight container in the refrigerator for up to 3 days.

Per Serving: Calories 354; Fat 7.9g; Sodium 704mg; Carbs 6g; Fiber 3.6g; Sugar 6g; Protein 18g

Cheese Cauliflower Bites

Prep time: 10 minutes. | Cooking time: 15 minutes. | Servings 4

1-pound cauliflower, grated
½ cup cheddar cheese, shredded
1-ounce butter, room temperature

Black pepper and salt, to taste
½ cup tortilla chips, crushed
2 eggs whisked

1. Thoroughly mix all the recipe ingredients in a mixing bowl. Shape the prepared mixture into bite-sized balls. 2. Cook on Air Fry mode and select level 3, cook the cauliflower balls at 350 degrees F/ 175 degrees C for about 13 minutes, turning them over halfway through the Cooking time. Bon appétit!
Per Serving: Calories 241; Fat 16.8 g; Sodium 225 mg; Carbs 8g; Fiber 0.4g; Sugar 1.1g; Protein 15.4g

Pancetta-Wrapped Shrimp

Prep time: 10 minutes. | Cooking time: 10 minutes. | Servings 4

12 shrimp, peeled and deveined
3 slices pancetta, cut into strips

2 tablespoons maple syrup
1 tablespoon Dijon mustard

1. Wrap the shrimp in the pancetta strips and toss them with the maple syrup and mustard. 2. Place the shrimp in a lightly greased air fryer cooking basket. 3. Cook on Air Fry mode and select level 3, cook the shrimp at 400 degrees F/ 200 degrees C for 6 minutes, tossing the basket halfway through the Cooking time. Bon appétit!
Per Serving: Calories 199; Fat 17.9g; Sodium 525mg; Carbs 1.1g; Fiber 0.3g; Sugar 0.6g; Protein 9.9g

Cheese Apple Pie Rolls

Prep time: 10 minutes. | Cooking time: 15 minutes. | Servings 4

6 ounces refrigerated crescent rolls
1 apple, peeled, cored, and grated
6 ounces cream cheese, crumbled

¼ cup brown sugar
1 teaspoon apple pie spice

1. Separate the prepared dough into rectangles. Mix the remaining recipe ingredients until well mixed. 2. Spread each rectangle with the cheese mixture; roll them up tightly. Place the rolls in the air fryer cooking basket. 3. Cook on Bake mode and select level 3, bake the rolls at 320 degrees F/ 160 degrees C for about 5 minutes. Turn them over and bake for a further 5 minutes.Bon appétit!
Per Serving: Calories 202; Fat 15.9g; Sodium 720 mg; Carbs 3.9g; Fiber 1.3g; Sugar 1.6g; Protein 12.4g

Homemade Roasted Mixed Nuts

Prep time: 5 minutes| Cook time: 20 minutes| Serves: 6

2 cups mixed nuts (walnuts, pecans, and/or almonds)
2 tablespoons egg white
1 teaspoon ground cinnamon

2 tablespoons sugar
1 teaspoon paprika

1. Install the wire rack on Level 3. Select the "AIR ROAST" function of Ninja Foodi Smart XL Pro Air Oven, set temperature to 300°F and time to 10 minutes. Select START/STOP to begin preheating. Spray the air fryer basket with olive oil. 2. In a mixing bowl, mix the nuts, egg white, cinnamon, sugar, and paprika, until the nuts are thoroughly coated. 3. Place the nuts in the greased air fryer basket; set the timer and roast for 10 minutes. 4.Pour the nuts into a bowl, and serve.
Per Serving: Calories 232; Fat 21g; Sodium 6mg; Carbs 10g; Fiber 3g; Sugar 5g; Protein 6g

Sweet Potato Fries

Prep time: 10 minutes| Cook time: 20 minutes| Serves: 2 to 3

1 large sweet potato (about 1 pound)
1 teaspoon vegetable or canola oil
Sweet & Spicy Dipping Sauce:
¼ cup light mayonnaise
1 tablespoon spicy brown mustard

salt

1 tablespoon sweet Thai chili sauce
½ teaspoon sriracha sauce

1. Scrub the sweet potato well and cut it into ¼-inch French fries. (A mandolin slicer can really help with this.)2. Select Level 3. Select the "AIR FRY" function of Ninja Foodi Smart XL Pro Air Oven, set temperature to 250°F and time to 10 minutes. Select START/STOP to begin preheating. 3. Toss the sweet potato sticks with the oil and transfer them to the air fryer basket. Air-fry = for 10 minutes, shaking the basket several times during the cooking process for even cooking. Toss the fries with salt, increase the air fryer temperature to 400°F and air-fry for another 10 minutes, shaking the basket several times during the cooking process. 4. For dipping, mix all the ingredients in a bowl and stir until combined. 5. Serve the sweet potato fries warm with the dipping sauce on the side.
Per Serving: Calories 130; Fat 1g; Sodium 336mg; Carbs 28g; Fiber 4g; Sugar 9g; Protein 3g

Lemony Ricotta with Capers

Prep time: 5 minutes| Cook time: 10 minutes| Serves: 4 to6

1½ cups ricotta cheese
zest of 1 lemon,
1 teaspoon chopped rosemary
pinch red pepper flakes

2 tablespoons capers, rinsed
2 tablespoons extra-virgin olive oil
salt and freshly ground black pepper
1 tablespoon grated Parmesan cheese

1. Select Level 3. Select the "AIR FRY" function of Ninja Foodi Smart XL Pro Air Oven, set temperature to 390°F and time to 10 minutes. Select START/STOP to begin preheating. 2. Combine the cheese with lemon zest, rosemary, red pepper flakes, capers, olive oil, salt and pepper and whisk together well. Transfer the cheese mixture to a 7-inch pie dish and place the pie dish in the air fryer basket. 3. Air-fry the ricotta for 8 to 10 minutes, or until the top is nicely browned in spots. 4. Remove the pie dish from the air fryer and immediately sprinkle the Parmesan cheese on top. Drizzle with a bit of olive oil and add some freshly ground black pepper and lemon zest as garnish. Serve warm with pita breads or crostini.
Per Serving: Calories 150; Fat 13g; Sodium 398mg; Carbs 2g; Fiber 0g; Sugar 0g; Protein 7g

Easy Ranch Roasted Chickpeas

Prep time: 4 minutes| Cook time: 10 minutes| Serves: 4

1 (15-ounce) can chickpeas, drained and rinsed
1 tablespoon olive oil
3 tablespoons ranch seasoning mix

1 teaspoon salt
2 tablespoons freshly squeezed lemon juice

1. Grease the air fryer basket with olive oil. 2. Using paper towels, pat the chickpeas dry. 3. In a bowl, add the chickpeas, oil, seasoning mix, salt, and lemon juice. 4. Put the chickpeas in the air fryer basket and spread them out in a single layer. Install the wire rack on Level 3. Select the "AIR ROAST" function of Ninja Foodi Smart XL Pro Air Oven, set temperature to 350°F and time to 4 minutes. Select START/STOP to begin preheating. 5. Set the timer and roast for 4 minutes. Remove the drawer and shake vigorously to redistribute the chickpeas so they cook evenly. Reset the timer and roast for 6 minutes more. 6. When the time is up, release the air fryer basket from the drawer and pour the chickpeas into a bowl. Season with additional salt, if desired. Enjoy!
Per Serving: Calories 144; Fat 5g; Sodium 891mg; Carbs 19g; Fiber 5g; Sugar 3g; Protein 6g

Spicy Chicken Cheese Balls

Prep time: 10 minutes| Cook time: 16 minutes| Serves: 8

8 ounces cream cheese, softened
2 cups grated pepper jack cheese
1 Jalapeño pepper, diced
2 scallions, minced
1 teaspoon paprika
2 teaspoons salt, divided

3 cups shredded cooked chicken
¼ cup all-purpose flour
2 eggs, lightly beaten
1 cup panko breadcrumbs
olive oil, in a spray bottle
salsa

1. Beat the cream cheese and add the pepper jack cheese, Jalapeño pepper, scallions, paprika and salt. Fold in the shredded chicken and combine well. Roll this mixture into 1-inch balls. 2. Place the flour into a shallow dish. Place the eggs into another shallow dish. Finally, combine the panko breadcrumbs and salt in a third dish. 3. Coat the chicken cheese balls with flour first, then dip them into the eggs and finally roll them in the panko breadcrumbs to coat all sides. Refrigerate for at least 30 minutes. 4. Select Level 3. Select the "AIR FRY" function of Ninja Foodi Smart XL Pro Air Oven, set temperature to 400°F and time to 8 minutes. Select START/STOP to begin preheating. 5. Spray the chicken cheese balls with oil and air-fry in batches for 8 minutes. Shake the basket a few times throughout the cooking process to help the balls brown evenly.6. Serve hot with salsa on the side.

Per Serving: Calories 310; Fat 20g; Sodium 614mg; Carbs 6g; Fiber 0g; Sugar 1g; Protein 25g

Fried Cheesy Ravioli with Marinara Sauce

Prep time: 7 minutes| Cook time: 14 minutes| Serves: 4 to 6

1-pound cheese ravioli, fresh or frozen
2 eggs, lightly beaten
1 cup plain breadcrumbs
½ teaspoon paprika
½ teaspoon dried oregano

½ teaspoon salt
grated Parmesan cheese
chopped fresh parsley
1 to 2 cups marinara sauce

1. Boil the salted water. Boil the ravioli and then drain. Let the cooked ravioli cool to a temperature where you can comfortably handle them. 2. Place the eggs into one dish. Combine the breadcrumbs, paprika, dried oregano and salt in the other dish. 3. Select Level 3. Select the "AIR FRY" function of Ninja Foodi Smart XL Pro Air Oven, set temperature to 380°F and time to 5 minutes. Select START/STOP to begin preheating. 4. Working with one at a time, dip the cooked ravioli into the egg, coating all sides. Then press the ravioli into the breadcrumbs, making sure that all sides are covered. Transfer the ravioli to the air fryer basket, cooking in batches, one layer at a time. Air-fry F for 7 minutes. 5. While the ravioli is air-frying, bring the marinara sauce to a simmer on the stovetop. Transfer to a small bowl. 6. Sprinkle a little Parmesan cheese and chopped parsley on top of the fried ravioli and serve warm with the marinara sauce on the side for dipping.

Per Serving: Calories 60; Fat 1g; Sodium 154mg; Carbs 9g; Fiber 1g; Sugar 3g; Protein 3g

Crispy Carrot Chips

Prep time: 5 minutes| Cook time: 6 to 8 minutes| Serves: 6

1 pound carrots, peeled and sliced ⅛ inch thick
2 tablespoons olive oil

1 teaspoon sea salt

1. In a bowl, combine the carrots, olive oil, and salt. Toss them together until the carrot slices are thoroughly coated with oil. 2. Place the carrot chips in the air fryer basket in a single layer. (You may have to bake the carrot chips in more than one batch.) 3. Install the wire rack on Level 3. Select the "BAKE" function of Ninja Foodi Smart XL Pro Air Oven, set temperature to 360°F and time to 3 minutes. Select START/STOP to begin preheating. Set the timer and bake for 3 minutes. Remove the air fryer drawer and shake to redistribute the chips for even cooking. Reset the timer and bake for 3 minutes more. 4. Check the carrot chips for doneness. If you like them extra crispy, give the basket another shake and cook them for another 1 to 2 minutes. 5. When the chips are done, release the air fryer basket from the drawer, pour the chips into a bowl, and serve.

Per Serving: Calories 71; Fat 5g; Sodium 364mg; Carbs 7g; Fiber 2g; Sugar 4g; Protein 1g

No-Corn Cheesy Hot Dogs

Prep time: 10 minutes| Cook time: 10 minutes| Serves: 4

1¾ cups shredded mozzarella cheese (about 7 ounces)
2 tablespoons unsalted butter
1 large egg
For Serving:
Prepared yellow mustard

¾ cup blanched almond flour
⅛ teaspoon fine sea salt
4 hot dogs

No-sugar or reduced-sugar ketchup

1. **Make the dough:** Place the mozzarella cheese and butter in a large bowl and microwave for 2 minutes, until the cheese melted. Stir well. Add the egg and, using a hand mixer, combine well. Add the almond flour and salt and combine well with the mixer. 2. Lay a piece of parchment paper on the countertop, spray it with avocado oil, and place the dough on it. Knead for about 3 minutes. The dough should be thick yet pliable. 3. Spray the air fryer basket with avocado oil. Select Level 3. Select the "AIR FRY" function of Ninja Foodi Smart XL Pro Air Oven, set temperature to 390°F and time to 5 minutes. Select START/STOP to begin preheating. 4. Separate the dough into 4 equal portions. Pat each portion out with your hands to form a small oval, about 6 inches long and 2 inches wide. 5. Place one hot dog in each oval and form the dough around each hot dog using your hands. Place the dogs in the air fryer basket, leaving space between them, and cook for 8 minutes, or until golden brown, flipping halfway through. Drizzle with yellow mustard and serve with ketchup on the side, if desired. 6. Store leftovers in an airtight container in the refrigerator for up to 3 days.

Per Serving: Calories 354; Fat 7.9g; Sodium 704mg; Carbs 6g; Fiber 3.6g; Sugar 6g; Protein 18g

Parmesan Eggplant Fries

Prep time: 5 minutes| Cook time: 18 minutes| Serves: 6

½ cup all-purpose flour
salt and freshly ground black pepper
2 eggs, beaten
1 cup seasoned breadcrumbs
1 large eggplant

8 ounces mozzarella cheese
olive oil, in a spray bottle
grated Parmesan cheese
1 (14-ounce) jar marinara sauce

1. Place the flour in a shallow dish and spice with salt and freshly ground black pepper. Put the eggs in the second shallow dish. Place the breadcrumbs in the third shallow dish. 2. Peel the eggplant and then slice it vertically into long ½-inch thick slices. Slice the mozzarella cheese into ½-inch thick slices and make a mozzarella sandwich, using the eggplant as the bread. Slice the eggplant-mozzarella sandwiches into rectangular strips about 1-inch by 3½-inches. 3. Coat the eggplant strips carefully, holding the sandwich together with your fingers. Dredge with flour first, then dip them into the eggs, and finally place them into the breadcrumbs. Pat the crumbs onto the eggplant strips and then coat them in the egg and breadcrumbs one more time, pressing gently with your hands so the crumbs stick evenly. 4. Select Level 3. Select the "AIR FRY" function of Ninja Foodi Smart XL Pro Air Oven, set temperature to 400°F and time to 9 minutes. Select START/STOP to begin preheating. 5. Spray the eggplant fries on all sides with olive oil, and transfer one layer at a time to the air-fryer basket. Air-fry in batches for 9 minutes, turning and rotating halfway through the cooking time. Spray the eggplant strips with additional oil when you turn them over.6. While the fries are cooking, gently warm the marinara sauce on the stovetop in a small saucepan.7. Serve eggplant fries fresh out of the air fryer with a little Parmesan cheese grated on top and the warmed marinara sauce on the side.

Per Serving: Calories 210; Fat 11g; Sodium 268mg; Carbs 16g; Fiber 4g; Sugar 7g; Protein 12g

Tomato and Basil Bruschetta

Prep time: 5 minutes| Cook time: 3 minutes| Serves: 6

4 tomatoes, diced
⅓ cup fresh basil, shredded
¼ cup shredded Parmesan cheese
1 tablespoon minced garlic
1 tablespoon balsamic vinegar

1 teaspoon olive oil
1 teaspoon salt
1 teaspoon freshly ground black pepper
1 loaf French bread

1. In a bowl, add the tomatoes and basil. 2. Mix in the Parmesan cheese, garlic, vinegar, olive oil, salt, and pepper. 3. Let the tomato mixture sit and marinate, while you prepare the bread.4. Select Level 3. Select the "AIR FRY" function of Ninja Foodi Smart XL Pro Air Oven, set temperature to 250°F and time to 3 minutes. Select START/STOP to begin preheating. Grease the air fryer basket with olive oil. 5. Cut the bread into 1-inch-thick slices. 6. Place the slices in the greased air fryer basket in a single layer. 7. Spray the top of the bread with olive oil. 8. Set the temperature to 250°F. Set the timer and coo for 3 minutes. 9. Using tongs, remove the bread slices from the air fryer and place a spoonful of the bruschetta topping on each piece.
Per Serving: Calories 258; Fat 3g; Sodium 826mg; Carbs 47g; Fiber 3g; Sugar 4g; Protein 11g

Sweet and Salty Snack

Prep time: 10 minutes| Cook time: 20 minutes| Serves: 10

1 teaspoon salt
2 cups sesame sticks
½ cup honey
3 tablespoons butter, melted
1 cup pepitas

2 cups granola
1 cup cashews
2 cups crispy corn puff cereal
2 cups mini pretzel crisps
1 cup dried cherries

1. Combine the honey, butter and salt in a small bowl or measuring cup and stir until combined. 2. Mix the sesame sticks, pepitas, granola, cashews, corn puff cereal and pretzel crisps in a large bowl. Pour the honey mixture and toss to combine. 3. Select the "AIR FRY" function of Ninja Foodi Smart XL Pro Air Oven, set temperature to 370°F and time to 10 minutes. Select START/STOP to begin preheating. 4. Place half the mixture in the air fryer basket. Slide basket into rails of Level 3 and air-fry for 10 to 12 minutes, or until the snack mix is lightly toasted. Toss the basket several times throughout the process so that the mixture cooks evenly and doesn't get too dark on top. 5. Transfer the snack mix to a cookie sheet and let it cool completely. Mix in the dried cherries and store the mix in an airtight container for up to a week or two.
Per Serving: Calories 270; Fat 12g; Sodium 633mg; Carbs 35g; Fiber 3g; Sugar 15g; Protein 6g

Mozzarella Sticks

Prep time: 10 minutes| Cook time: 8 minutes| Serves: 6

1 (12-count) package mozzarella sticks
1 (8-ounce) package crescent roll dough
3 tablespoons unsalted butter, melted

¼ cup panko bread crumbs
Marinara sauce, for dipping

1. Grease the air fryer basket with olive oil. 2. Cut each cheese stick into thirds. 3. Unroll the crescent roll dough. With sharp knife, cut the dough into 36 even pieces. 4. Wrap each small cheese stick in a piece of dough. Make sure that the dough is wrapped tightly around the cheese. Close the dough by pinching them together at both ends, and pinch along the seam to ensure that the dough is completely sealed. 5. Using tongs, dip the wrapped cheese sticks in the melted butter, then dip the cheese sticks in the panko bread crumbs. 6. Place the cheese sticks in the greased air fryer basket in a single layer. (You may have to cook the cheese sticks in more than one batch.)7. Install the wire rack on Level 3. Select the "BAKE" function of Ninja Foodi Smart XL Pro Air Oven, set temperature to 370°F and time to 5 minutes. Select START/STOP to begin preheating. Set the timer and bake for 5 minutes. After 5 minutes, the tops should be golden brown. 8. Using tongs, flip the cheese sticks and bake for another 3 minutes, or until golden brown on all sides. 9. Plate, serve with the marinara sauce and enjoy!
Per Serving: Calories 348; Fat 23g; Sodium 811mg; Carbs 21g; Fiber 1g; Sugar 3g; Protein 17g

Air Fried Pita Chips

Prep time: 5 minutes| Cook time: 6 minutes| Serves: 4

2 pieces whole wheat pita bread
3 tablespoons olive oil
1 teaspoon freshly squeezed lemon juice

1 teaspoon salt
1 teaspoon dried basil
1 teaspoon garlic powder

1. Grease the air fryer basket with olive oil. 2. Use a pair of kitchen shears or a pizza cutter, cut the pita bread into small wedges. 3. Place the wedges in a small mixing bowl and add the olive oil, lemon juice, salt, dried basil, and garlic powder. 4. Mix well, coating each wedge. 5. Place the seasoned pita wedges in the greased air fryer basket in a single layer, being careful not to overcrowd them. (You may have to bake the pita chips in more than one batch.) 6. Install the wire rack on Level 3. Select the "BAKE" function of Ninja Foodi Smart XL Pro Air Oven, set temperature to 350°F and time to 6 minutes. Select START/STOP to begin preheating. Set the timer and bake for 6 minutes. Every 2 minutes or so, remove the drawer and shake the pita chips so they redistribute in the basket for even cooking. 7. Serve with your choice of dip or alone as a tasty snack.
Per Serving: Calories 178; Fat 11g; Sodium 752mg; Carbs 18g; Fiber 3g; Sugar 1g; Protein 3g

Healthy Hot Dog Buns

Prep time: 10 minutes| Cook time: 25 minutes| Serves: 1

1½ cups blanched almond flour
¼ cup plus 1 tablespoon psyllium husk powder
2 teaspoons baking powder
1 teaspoon fine sea salt

2½ tablespoons apple cider vinegar
3 large egg whites
1 cup boiling water

1. Spray a 7-inch pie pan or a casserole dish that will fit inside your air fryer with avocado oil. Select Level 3. Select the "AIR FRY" function of Ninja Foodi Smart XL Pro Air Oven, set temperature to 325°F and time to 25 minutes. Select START/STOP to begin preheating. 2. In a medium-sized bowl, mix together the flour, psyllium husk powder, baking powder, and salt until well combined. Add the vinegar and egg whites and stir until a thick dough forms. Add the boiling water and mix until well combined. Let sit for 1 to 2 minutes, until the dough firms up. 3. Divide the dough into 8 equal-sized balls. Form each ball into a hot dog shape that's about 1-inch wide and 3½ inches long. Place the buns in the greased pie pan, spacing them about 1 inch apart. 4. Place the buns in the air fryer and cook for 15 minutes, then flip the buns over. Cook for another 5 to 10 minutes, until the buns are puffed up and cooked through and a toothpick inserts in the center of a bun comes out clean. 5. Store leftovers in an airtight container in the fridge for up to 5 days or in the freezer for up to a month.
Per Serving: Calories 354; Fat 7.9g; Sodium 704mg; Carbs 6g; Fiber 3.6g; Sugar 6g; Protein 18g

Seasoned Sausage Rolls

Prep time: 5 minutes| Cook time: 5 minutes| Serves: 6

For the Seasoning:
2 tablespoons sesame seeds
1½ teaspoons poppy seeds
1½ teaspoons dried minced onion
For the Sausages:
1 (8-ounce) package crescent roll dough
To Make the Seasoning:
In a bowl, combine the sesame seeds, poppy seeds, onion, salt,
To Make the Sausages:

1 teaspoon salt
1 teaspoon dried minced garlic

1 (12-ounce) package mini smoked sausages (cocktail franks)

and garlic and set aside.

1. Select Level 3. Select the "AIR FRY" function of Ninja Foodi Smart XL Pro Air Oven, set temperature to 330°F and time to 5 minutes. Select START/STOP to begin preheating. Grease the air fryer basket with olive oil. 2. Remove the crescent dough from the package and lay it out on a cutting board. Separate the dough at the perforations. With sharp knife, cut each triangle of dough into fourths. 3. Drain the sausages and pat them dry with a paper towel. 4. Roll each sausage in a piece of dough. 5. Sprinkle seasoning on top of each roll. 6. Place the seasoned sausage rolls into the greased air fryer basket in a single layer. Air fry it for 5 minutes.
Per Serving: Calories 344; Fat 26g; Sodium 1145mg; Carbs 17g; Fiber 1g; Sugar 3g; Protein 10g

Chapter 7 Desserts

Boston Cream Donut

Prep time: 10 minutes. | Cooking time: 12 minutes. | Servings: 12

1½ cups bread flour
1 teaspoon active dry yeast
1 tablespoon sugar
¼ teaspoon salt
½ cup warm milk
Custard filling:
1 (4-ounce) box French vanilla instant pudding mix
¾ cup whole milk
Chocolate glaze:
1 cup chocolate chips

½ teaspoon pure vanilla extract
2 egg yolks
2 tablespoons butter, melted
Vegetable oil

¼ cup heavy cream

⅓ cup heavy cream

1. In the bowl of a standing mixer, mix the flour, yeast, sugar, and salt. Add the butter, milk, vanilla, and egg yolks. Mix until a ball of the prepared dough begins to form. Place the prepared dough on a floured board and give it a 2-minute hand kneading. The prepared dough should be formed into a ball, placed in an appropriate oiled bowl, covered with a clean kitchen towel, and leave it to rise for one to eleven and a half hours. 2. When the prepared dough has risen, punch it down and roll it into a 24-inch log. Cut the prepared dough into 24 pieces and roll each piece into a ball. Place the prepared dough balls on a suitable baking sheet and let them rise for another 30 minutes.3. Cook on Air Fry mode. Pre-heat the Ninja Foodi Smart Xl Pro air fryer to 400 degrees F/ 200 degrees C. Select Level "3" and set the time on your Ninja Foodi Smart XL Pro Air Fryer Oven to 4 minutes. Press Start/ Pause to begin preheating. 4. Insert the basket in the level 3 of the Ninja Foodi Smart XL Pro Oven. Spray or brush the prepared dough balls lightly with vegetable oil and air-fry eight at a time for 4 minutes.5. To make the filling, use an electric hand mixer to beat the French vanilla pudding, milk and ¼ cup of heavy cream for 2 minutes.6. Put the chocolate chips in a medium-sized bowl to start the chocolate glaze. Over the chocolate chips, pour the heavy cream that has been heated on the stovetop to a boil. Stir the glaze and chips together until they are melted.7. Place the custard stuffing in a pastry bag with a large tip and use it to fill the donut holes. Use a sharp knife to make a hole in the donut hole's side. To accommodate the filling, wiggle the knife around. Squeeze the custard into the donut's center slowly by inserting the pastry bag tip into the hole. Pour the chocolate glaze over the top half of the doughnut, allowing any extra icing drip back into the bowl.
Per Serving: Calories 116; Fat 4.3 g; Sodium 28 mg; Carbs 32.9g; Fiber 2.5g; Sugar 29g; Protein 1.6g

Berry Pies

Prep time: 10 minutes. | Cooking time: 30 minutes. | Servings: 4

¾ cup sugar
½ teaspoon ground cinnamon
1 tablespoon cornstarch
1 cup blueberries
1 cup blackberries

1 cup raspberries, divided
1 teaspoon water
1 package refrigerated pie dough (or your own homemade pie dough)
1 egg, beaten

1. Mix the sugar, cinnamon, and cornstarch in a suitable saucepan. Add the blueberries, blackberries, and ½ cup of the raspberries. Toss the berries gently to coat them evenly. Add the teaspoon of water to the saucepan and turn the stovetop on to medium-high heat, stirring occasionally. Once the berries break down, release their juice and start to simmer (about 5 minutes), simmer for another couple of minutes and then transfer the prepared mixture to a suitable bowl, stir in the remaining ½ cup of raspberries and let it cool. 2. Cut the pie dough into four 5-inch circles and four 6-inch circles. 3. Spread the 6-inch circles on a flat surface. Divide the berry filling between all four circles. Brush the perimeter of the prepared dough circles with a little water. Place the 5-inch circles on top of the filling and press the perimeter of the prepared dough circles to seal. Roll the edges of the bottom circle up over the top circle to make a crust around the filling. Press a fork around the crust to make decorative indentations and to seal the crust shut. Brush the pies with egg wash and topping with a little sugar. Poke a suitable hole in the center of each pie with a paring knife to vent the prepared dough. 4. Air-fry two pies at a time. Cook on Air Fry mode. Pre-heat the air fryer to 370 degrees F/ 185 degrees C. Select Level "3" and set the time on your Ninja Foodi Smart XL Pro Air Fryer Oven to 15 minutes. Press Start/Pause to begin preheating. Continue to the next step when it is done preheating. 5. Brush or spray its air fryer basket with oil and place the pies into the basket. insert the basket in the level 3 of the Ninja Foodi Smart XL Pro Oven. Air-fry for 9 minutes. Turn the pies over and air-fry for another 6 minutes. Serve warm or at room temperature.
Per Serving: Calories 551; Fat 29.3 g; Sodium 74 mg; Carbs 73.9g; Fiber 3.5g; Sugar 55.9g; Protein 5g

Sweet Chocolate Soufflés

Prep time: 10 minutes. | Cooking time: 14 minutes. | Servings: 2

Butter and sugar for greasing the ramekins
3 ounces semi-sweet chocolate, chopped
3 tablespoons sugar
¼ cup unsalted butter
2 eggs, separate yolks and white

½ teaspoon vanilla extract
2 tablespoons all-purpose flour
Powdered sugar, for dusting
Heavy cream, for serving
Butter and sugar two 6-ounce ramekins.

1. Melt the semi-sweet chocolate and butter in a bowl, in the microwave. 2. In a suitable bowl, beat the egg yolks. Stir in the sugar and the vanilla extract and beat well again. Drizzle in the melted chocolate and butter, mixing well. Add in the flour, combining until there are no lumps.3. Cook on Air Fry mode. Pre-heat the Ninja Foodi Smart Xl Pro air fryer to 330 degrees F/ 165 degrees C. Select Level "3" and set the time on your Ninja Foodi Smart XL Pro Air Fryer Oven to 10 minutes. Press Start/Pause to begin preheating. 4. In another suitable bowl, beat the egg whites to soft peak stage. 5. Add the whipped egg whites into the chocolate mixture gently and in stages.6. Transfer the prepared batter carefully to the buttered ramekins, leaving about ½-inch at the top. Place the ramekins into its air fryer basket and insert the basket in the level 3 of the Ninja Foodi Smart XL Pro Oven. Air-fry for 14 minutes. 7. Dust with sugar and serve with heavy cream

Per Serving: Calories 284; Fat 16g; Sodium 252mg; Carbs 31.6g; Fiber 0.9g; Sugar 6.6g; Protein 3.7g

Apple Crumble

Prep time: 10 minutes. | Cooking time: 50 minutes. | Servings: 6

4 apples, peeled and thinly sliced
2 tablespoons sugar
1 tablespoon flour
1 teaspoon ground cinnamon
Crumble topping:
¾ cup rolled oats
¼ cup sugar
⅓ cup flour

¼ teaspoon ground allspice
Healthy pinch ground nutmeg
10 caramel squares, cut into small pieces

¼ teaspoon ground cinnamon
6 tablespoons butter, melted

1. Mix the apples, sugar, flour, and spices in a suitable bowl and toss to coat. Add the caramel pieces and mix well. Pour the apple mixture into a 1-quart round baking dish that will fit in your air fryer basket (6-inch diameter). 2. To make the crumble topping, mix the rolled oats, sugar, flour and cinnamon in a suitable bowl. Add the melted butter and mix well. Top the apples with the crumble mixture. Cover this dish with foil and transfer the dish to its air fryer basket, lowering the dish into the basket using a sling made of aluminum foil. 3. Fold the ends of the aluminum foil over the top of the dish before returning the basket to the air fryer. 4. Cook on Air Fry mode. Pre-heat the air fryer to 330 degrees F/ 165 degrees C. Select Level "3" and set the time on your Ninja Foodi Smart XL Pro Air Fryer Oven to 25 minutes. Press Start/Pause to begin preheating. Continue to the next step when it is done preheating. 5. Insert the basket in the level 3 of the Ninja Foodi Smart XL Pro Oven. Air-fry at 330 degrees F/ 165 degrees C for 25 minutes. Remove the aluminum foil and continue to air-fry for another 25 minutes. Serve the crumble warm with whipped cream or vanilla ice cream, if desired.

Per Serving: Calories 426; Fat 36.3 g; Sodium 248 mg; Carbs 22.1g; Fiber 2g; Sugar 10.9g; Protein 6.6g

Currant Cookies

Prep time: 5 minutes. | Cooking time: 30 minutes. | Servings: 6

2 cups almond flour
2 teaspoons baking soda
½ cup ghee, melted

½ cup swerve
1 teaspoon vanilla extract
½ cup currants

1. In a suitable bowl, mix all the recipe ingredients and whisk well. 2. Spread this on a suitable baking sheet lined with parchment paper, put the pan in its air fryer basket. Insert its air fryer basket into the level 3 of the oven and close the door. Cook on "Bake" mode, select level 3, and set its temperature to 350 degrees F/175 degrees C for 30 minutes. 3. Cool down, cut into rectangles and serve.

Per Serving: Calories 276; Fat 2.1 g; Sodium 18 mg; Carbs 65.9g; Fiber 4.5g; Sugar 59g; Protein 2.6g

Chocolate Almond Cakes

Prep time: 10 minutes. | Cooking time: 13 minutes. | Servings: 3

Butter and flour for the ramekins
4 ounces dark chocolate, chopped
½ cup unsalted butter
2 eggs
2 egg yolks
¼ cup sugar
½ teaspoon pure vanilla extract

1 tablespoon all-purpose flour
3 tablespoons ground almonds
8 to 12 semisweet chocolate discs
Cocoa powder or powdered sugar, for dusting
Toasted almonds, chopped
Butter and flour three (6-ounce) ramekins.

1. Melt the dark chocolate and butter in a suitable by heating in the microwave. 2. In a suitable bowl, beat the eggs with egg yolks and sugar until smooth. 3. Add the vanilla extract. Whisk the chocolate mixture into the egg mixture. Stir in the flour and ground almonds.4. Transfer the prepared batter carefully to the buttered ramekins, filling halfway. Place two or three chocolate discs in the center of the prepared batter and then fill the ramekins to ½-inch below the top with the remaining batter. 5. Cook on Air Fry mode. Pre-heat the air fryer to 330 degrees F/ 165 degrees C. Select Level "3" and set the time on your Ninja Foodi Smart XL Pro Air Fryer Oven to 13 minutes. Press Start/Pause to begin preheating. Continue to the next step when it is done preheating.6. Place the ramekins into its air fryer basket, insert the basket in the level 3 of the Ninja Foodi Smart XL Pro Oven. and air-fry at 330 degrees F/ 165 degrees C for 13 minutes. 7. Serve.
Per Serving: Calories 477; Fat 13.3 g; Sodium 128 mg; Carbs 89.5g; Fiber 6.5g; Sugar 59.2g; Protein 5.4g

Exquisite Puff Pastry Apples

Prep time: 10 minutes. | Cooking time: 10 minutes. | Servings: 4

3 Rome or gala apples, peeled
2 tablespoons sugar
1 teaspoon all-purpose flour
1 teaspoon ground cinnamon
⅛ teaspoon ground ginger
Pinch ground nutmeg

1 sheet puff pastry
1 tablespoon butter, cut into 4 pieces
1 egg, beaten
Vegetable oil
Vanilla ice cream
Caramel sauce

1. Remove the cores from the apples by cutting the four sides off the apple around the core. Slice the pieces of apple into thin half-moons, about ¼-inch thick. Mix the sugar, flour, cinnamon, ginger, and nutmeg in a suitable bowl. Add the apples to this bowl and gently toss until the apples are evenly coated with the spice mixture. Set aside.2. Cut the puff pastry sheet into a 12- by 12-inch square. Then quarter the sheet into four 6-inch squares. 3. Save any remaining pastry for decorating the apples at the end.4. Divide the spiced apples between the four puff pastry squares, stacking the apples in the center of each square and placing them flat on top of each other in a circle. Top the apples with a piece of the butter.5. Brush the edges of the pastry with the egg wash. Bring the four corners of the pastry together, wrapping them around the apple slices and pinching them at the top in the style of a "beggars purse" appetizer. Fold the ends of the pastry corners down onto the apple making them look like leaves. Brush the entire apple with the egg wash.6. Using the leftover dough, make leaves to decorate the apples. Cut out 8 leaf shapes, about 1½-inches long, "drawing" the leaf veins on the pastry leaves with a paring knife. Place 2 leaves on the top of each apple, tucking the ends of the leaves under the pastry in the center of the apples. Brush the top of the leaves with additional egg wash. Sprinkle the entire apple with some granulated sugar.7. Spray or brush the inside of its air fryer basket with oil. Cook on Air Fry mode. Pre-heat the air fryer to 350 degrees F/ 175 degrees C. Select Level "3" and set the time on your Ninja Foodi Smart XL Pro Air Fryer Oven to 10 minutes. Press Start/Pause to begin preheating. Continue to the next step when it is done preheating.8. Place the apples in the basket, insert the basket in the level 3 of the Ninja Foodi Smart XL Pro Oven. 9. Air-fry for 6 minutes. Carefully turn the apples over – it's easiest to remove one apple, then flip the others over and finally return the last apple to the air fryer. Air-fry for an additional 4 minutes.10. Serve the puff pastry apples warm with vanilla ice cream and drizzle with some caramel sauce.
Per Serving: Calories 148; Fat 0.3 g; Sodium 3 mg; Carbs 38.9g; Fiber 0.5g; Sugar 33.9g; Protein 0.6g

Carrot Cake With Icing

Prep time: 10 minutes. | Cooking time: 55 minutes. | Servings: 6

1¼ cups all-purpose flour
1 teaspoon baking powder
½ teaspoon baking soda
1 teaspoon ground cinnamon
¼ teaspoon ground nutmeg
¼ teaspoon salt
For the icing:
8 ounces cream cheese, softened
8 tablespoons butter (4 ounces or 1 stick), softened at room temperature

2 cups grated carrot (about 3 to 4 medium carrots or 2 large)
¾ cup granulated sugar
¼ cup brown sugar
2 eggs
¾ cup canola or vegetable oil

1 cup powdered sugar
1 teaspoon pure vanilla extract
Grease a 7-inch cake pan.

1. Mix the flour, baking powder, baking soda, cinnamon, nutmeg and salt in a suitable bowl. Add the grated carrots and toss well. In a separate bowl, beat the sugars and eggs until light and frothy. Drizzle in the oil, beating constantly. Fold the egg mixture into the dry ingredients until everything is just mixed and you no longer see any traces of flour. Pour the prepared batter into the cake pan and wrap the pan completely in greased aluminum foil. 2. Lower the cake pan into its air fryer basket using a sling made of aluminum foil. Fold both the ends of the aluminum foil into the air fryer, letting them rest on top of the cake. 3. Cook on Air Fry mode. Pre-heat the air fryer to 350 degrees F/ 175 degrees C. Select Level "3" and set the time on your Ninja Foodi Smart XL Pro Air Fryer Oven to 40 minutes. Press Start/Pause to begin preheating. Continue to the next step when it is done preheating.4. Insert the basket in the level 3 of the Ninja Foodi Smart XL Pro Oven. Air-fry for 40 minutes. 5. While the cake is cooking, beat the cream cheese, butter, powdered sugar and vanilla extract using a hand mixer or food processor (or a lot of elbow grease!).6. Remove the cake's pan from the air fryer and let the cake cool in the cake pan for 10 minutes or so. Frost the cake with the cream cheese icing and serve.
Per Serving: Calories 276; Fat 2.1 g; Sodium 18 mg; Carbs 65.9g; Fiber 4.5g; Sugar 59g; Protein 2.6g

Nutella Torte

Prep time: 10 minutes. | Cooking time: 55 minutes. | Servings: 6

¼ cup unsalted butter, softened
½ cup sugar
2 eggs
1 teaspoon vanilla
1¼ cups Nutella (or other chocolate hazelnut spread), divided

¼ cup flour
1 teaspoon baking powder
¼ teaspoon salt
Dark chocolate fudge topping
Coarsely chopped toasted hazelnuts

1. Beat the butter and sugar with an electric hand mixer until light and fluffy. Add the eggs, vanilla, and ¾ cup of the Nutella and mix until mixed. Mix the flour, baking powder and salt together, and add these dry ingredients to the butter mixture, beating for 1 minute. 2. Grease a 7-inch cake pan with butter and then line the bottom of the pan with a circle of parchment paper. Grease the parchment paper circle as well. Pour the prepared batter into the prepared cake pan and wrap the pan completely with aluminum foil. Lower the pan into its air fryer basket with an aluminum sling. Fold the ends of the aluminum foil over the top of the dish before returning the basket to the air fryer. 3. Cook on Air Fry mode. Pre-heat the air fryer to 350 degrees F/ 175 degrees C. Select Level "3" and set the time on your Ninja Foodi Smart XL Pro Air Fryer Oven to 55 minutes. Press Start/Pause to begin preheating. Continue to the next step when it is done preheating. 4. Insert the basket in the level 3 of the Ninja Foodi Smart XL Pro Oven. Air-fry for 30 minutes. Remove the foil and air-fry for another 25 minutes. 5. Remove the cake from air fryer and let it cool for 10 minutes. Invert the cake onto a plate, remove the parchment paper and invert the cake back onto a serving platter. While the cake is still warm, spread the remaining ½ cup of Nutella® over the top of the cake. Melt the dark chocolate fudge in the microwave for about 10 seconds so it melts enough to be pourable. Drizzle the sauce on top of the cake in a zigzag motion. Turn the cake 90 degrees and drizzle more sauce in zigzags perpendicular to the first zigzags. Garnish the edges of the torte with the toasted hazelnuts and serve.
Per Serving: Calories 116; Fat 2.3 g; Sodium 15 mg; Carbs 18.9g; Fiber 4.5g; Sugar 2.2g; Protein 6g

Orange Butter Cake

Prep time: 10 minutes. | Cooking time: 77 minutes. | Servings: 6

Crust layer:
½ cup flour
¼ cup sugar
½ teaspoon baking powder
⅛ teaspoon salt

Gooey butter layer:
8 ounces cream cheese, softened
4 ounces (1 stick) unsalted European style butter, melted
2 eggs

Garnish:
Powdered sugar

2 ounces (½ stick) unsalted European style butter, melted
1 egg
1 teaspoon orange extract
2 tablespoons orange zest

2 teaspoons orange extract
2 tablespoons orange zest
4 cups powdered sugar

Orange slices

1. Grease a 7-inch cake pan and line the bottom with baking paper. Mix the flour, sugar, baking powder and salt in a suitable bowl. Add the melted butter, egg, orange extract and orange zest. Mix well and press this mixture into the bottom of the greased cake pan. Lower the pan into the basket using an aluminum foil sling (fold a piece of aluminum foil into a strip about 2-inches wide by 24-inches long). Fold the ends of the foil over the top of the dish before returning the basket to the air fryer. Air-fry uncovered for 8 minutes. 2. To make the gooey butter layer, beat the cream cheese, melted butter, eggs, orange extract and orange zest in a suitable bowl using an electric hand mixer. Add the powdered sugar in stages, beat until smooth with each addition. Pour this mixture on top of the baked crust in the cake pan. Wrap the pan with a piece of greased aluminum foil, tenting the top of the foil to leave a little room for the cake to rise. 3. Select Air Fry mode, pre-heat the air fryer to 350 degrees F/ 175 degrees C. Select Level "3" and set the time on your Ninja Foodi Smart XL Pro Air Fryer Oven to 60 minutes. Press Start/Pause to begin preheating. Continue to the next step when it is done preheating. 4. Place the pan in the oven and air-fry for 60 minutes. Remove the aluminum foil and insert the basket in the level 3 of the Ninja Foodi Smart XL Pro Oven. air-fry for an additional 17 minutes. 5. Let the cake cool inside the pan for at least 10 minutes. Then, run a butter knife around the cake and let the cake cool completely in the pan. When cooled, run the butter knife around the edges of the cake again and invert it onto a plate and then back onto a serving platter. Sprinkle the powdered sugar over the top of the cake and garnish with orange slices.

Per Serving: Calories 399; Fat 13 g; Sodium 626 mg; Carbs 52.9g; Fiber 8.8g; Sugar 3.9g; Protein 19.6g

Bananas Bread Pudding

Prep time: 10 minutes. | Cooking time: 50 minutes. | Servings: 4

½ cup brown sugar
3 eggs
¾ cup half and half
1 teaspoon pure vanilla extract

6 cups cubed kings Hawaiian bread (½-inch cubes), ½ pound
2 bananas, sliced
1 cup caramel sauce, plus more for serving

1. Mix the brown sugar, eggs, half and half and vanilla extract in a suitable bowl, whisking until the sugar has dissolved and the prepared mixture is smooth. Stir in the cubed bread and toss to coat all the cubes evenly. Let the bread sit for 10 minutes to absorb the liquid. 2. Mix the sliced bananas and caramel sauce in a separate bowl.3. Fill the bottom of 4 (8-ounce) greased ramekins with half the bread cubes. Divide the caramel and bananas between the ramekins, spooning them on top of the bread cubes. Top with the remaining bread cubes and wrap each ramekin with aluminum foil, tenting the foil at the top to leave some room for the bread to puff up during the cooking process. 4. Cook on Air Fry mode, pre-heat the Ninja Foodi Smart Xl Pro air fryer to 350 degrees F/ 175 degrees C. Select Level "3" and set the time on your Ninja Foodi Smart XL Pro Air Fryer Oven to 25 minutes. Press Start/Pause to begin preheating. 5. Insert the basket in the level 3 of the Ninja Foodi Smart XL Pro Oven. Air-fry two bread puddings at a time for 25 minutes. Let the puddings cool a little and serve warm with additional caramel sauce drizzled on top. 6. Serve

Per Serving: Calories 386; Fat 10.3 g; Sodium 238 mg; Carbs 72.9g; Fiber 4.5g; Sugar 59g; Protein 2.6g

Cream Cheesecake

Prep time: 10 minutes. | Cooking time: 2 minutes. | Servings: 2

Ingredients
½ cup erythritol
½ cup almond flour
½ teaspoon vanilla extract

2 tablespoons erythritol
4 tablespoons divided heavy cream
8 ounces cream cheese

1. Allow the cream cheese to soften then incorporate with the 2 tablespoons heavy cream, vanilla, and ½ cup erythritol until smooth and mixed. 2. Transfer the prepared mixture onto a suitable baking sheet lined with parchment paper then place in the freezer until firm. 3. Using a medium sized bowl, then add in the almond flour and tablespoons erythritol then mix together. 4. dip the cheesecake bites into the remaining heavy cream then run through the flour mixture. 5. Select Air Fry mode. Spread the bites into the fryer basket and insert the basket in the level 3 of the Ninja Foodi Smart XL Pro Oven. air fry at 300 degrees F/ 150 degrees C. and set the time on your Ninja Foodi Smart XL Pro Air Fryer Oven to 2 minutes. 6. Serve and enjoy as desired.
Per Serving: Calories 391; Fat 24g; Sodium 142mg; Carbs 38.5g; Fiber 3.5g; Sugar 21g; Protein 6.6g

Hazelnut Cookies

Prep time: 25 minutes. | Cooking time: 11 minutes. | Servings: 6

1 tablespoon flaxseeds
¼ cup flax meal
½ cup coconut flour
½ teaspoon baking powder
1 ounces hazelnuts, chopped

1 teaspoon apple cider vinegar
3 tablespoons coconut cream
1 tablespoon butter, softened
3 teaspoons Splenda
Cooking spray

1. Put the flax meal in the bowl. Add flax seeds, coconut flour, baking powder, apple cider vinegar, and Splenda. Stir the prepared mixture gently with the help of the fork and add butter, coconut cream, hazelnuts, and knead the non-sticky dough. If the prepared dough is not sticky enough, then add more coconut cream. 2. Make the big ball from the prepared dough and put it in the freezer for 10-15 minutes. 3. After this, Select the Air Fry mode. Set the Ninja Foodi Smart XL Pro temperature to 365 degrees F/ 185 degrees C. Select Level "3" and set the time on your Ninja Foodi Smart XL Pro Air Fryer Oven to 10 minutes. Press Start/Pause to begin preheating. Continue to the next step when it is done preheating. 4. Make the small balls (cookies) from the flax meal dough and press them gently. Spray its air fryer basket with cooking spray from inside. Spread the cookies in its air fryer basket in one layer (cook 3-4 cookies per one time) and Insert its air fryer basket into the level 3 of the oven and close the door. cook them for 11 minutes. 5. Then transfer the cooked cookies on the plate and cool them completely. Repeat the same steps with remaining uncooked cookies. 6. Store the cookies in the glass jar with the closed lid.
Per Serving: Calories 426; Fat 36.3 g; Sodium 248 mg; Carbs 22.1g; Fiber 2g; Sugar 10.9g; Protein 6.6g

Banana S'mores

Prep time: 10 minutes. | Cooking time: 6 minutes. | Servings: 4

4 bananas
3 tablespoons mini semi-sweet chocolate chips
3 tablespoons mini peanut butter chips

3 tablespoons mini marshmallows
3 tablespoons graham cracker cereal

1. Cut into the unpeeled bananas lengthwise along the inside of the curve to make a pocket 2. Fill each banana pocket with chocolate chips, peanut butter chips and marshmallows and poke the graham cracker cereal into the filling. 3. Cook on Air Fry mode, pre-heat the air fryer to 400 degrees F/ 200 degrees C. Select Level "3" and set the time on your Ninja Foodi Smart XL Pro Air Fryer Oven to 6 minutes. Press Start/Pause to begin preheating. Continue to the next step when it is done preheating. 4. Place the bananas in its air fryer basket, resting them on the side of the basket against each other so that they remain upright with the filling facing up. Insert the basket in the level 3 of the Ninja Foodi Smart XL Pro Oven. Air-fry for 6 minutes, until the bananas are soft to the touch, the chocolate and marshmallows have melted and toasted. Serve.
Per Serving: Calories 416; Fat 8.3 g; Sodium 208 mg; Carbs 22.9g; Fiber 0.5g; Sugar 19g; Protein 60.6g

Clove Flaxseed Crackers

Prep time: 20 minutes. | Cooking time: 33 minutes. | Servings: 8

1 cup almond flour
1 teaspoon xanthan gum
1 teaspoon flax meal
½ teaspoon salt
1 teaspoon baking powder

1 teaspoon lemon juice
½ teaspoon ground clove
2 tablespoons erythritol
1 egg, beaten
3 tablespoons coconut oil, softened

1. In the mixing bowl mix up almond flour, xanthan gum, flax meal, salt, baking powder, and ground clove. 2. Add erythritol, lemon juice, egg, and coconut oil. Stir the prepared mixture gently with the help of the fork. 3 Then knead the prepared mixture till you get a soft dough. Line the chopping board with parchment. 4. Put the prepared dough on the parchment and roll it up in a thin layer. Cut the thin dough into squares (crackers). 5. Select the Air Fry mode. Set the Ninja Foodi Smart XL Pro temperature to 360 degrees F/ 180 degrees C. Select Level "3" and set the time on your Ninja Foodi Smart XL Pro Air Fryer Oven to 11 minutes. Press Start/Pause to begin preheating. Continue to the next step when it is done preheating. 6. Line its air fryer basket with baking paper. Put the prepared crackers in its air fryer basket in one layer. Insert its air fryer basket into the level 3 of the oven and close the door. And cook them for 11 minutes until the crackers are dry and light brown. 7. Repeat the same steps with remaining uncooked crackers.

Per Serving: Calories 56; Fat 4.3 g; Sodium 21 mg; Carbs 2.9g; Fiber 0.3g; Sugar 3.9g; Protein 0.6g

Dark Chocolate Fudge

Prep time: 15 minutes. | Cooking time: 30 minutes. | Servings:8

½ cup butter, melted
1 ounces dark chocolate, chopped, melted
2 tablespoons cocoa powder
3 tablespoons coconut flour

1 teaspoon vanilla extract
2 eggs, beaten
3 tablespoons Splenda
Cooking spray

1. In the bowl mix up melted butter and dark chocolate. Then add vanilla extract, eggs, and cocoa powder. Stir the prepared mixture until smooth and add Splenda, and coconut flour. Stir it again until smooth. 2. Then Select the Air Fry mode. Set the Ninja Foodi Smart XL Pro temperature to 325 degrees F/ 160 degrees C. Select Level "3" and set the time on your Ninja Foodi Smart XL Pro Air Fryer Oven to 30 minutes. Press Start/Pause to begin preheating. Continue to the next step when it is done preheating. 3. Line its air fryer basket with baking paper and spray it with cooking spray. 4. Pour the fudge mixture in its air fryer basket, flatten it gently with the help of the spatula. Insert its air fryer basket into the level 3 of the oven and close the door. Cook the fudge for 30 minutes. 5. Then cut it on the serving squares and cool the fudge completely.

Per Serving: Calories 416; Fat 8.3 g; Sodium 208 mg; Carbs 22.9g; Fiber 0.5g; Sugar 19g; Protein 6.6g

Delicious Mini Strawberry Pies

Prep time: 7 minutes| Cook time: 8 minutes| Serves: 8

1 cup sugar
¼ teaspoon ground cloves
1/8 teaspoon cinnamon powder
1 teaspoon vanilla extract

1 [12-oz.] can biscuit dough
12 oz. strawberry pie filling
¼ cup butter, melted

1. Install the wire rack on Level 3. Select the "BAKE" function of Ninja Foodi Smart XL Pro Air Oven, set temperature to 340°F and time to 10 minutes. Select START/STOP to begin preheating. In a bowl, mix together the sugar, cloves, cinnamon, and vanilla. 2. With a rolling pin, roll each piece of the biscuit dough into a flat, round circle. 3. Spoon an equal amount of the strawberry pie filling onto the center of each biscuit. 4. Roll up the dough. Dip the biscuits into the melted butter and coat them with the sugar mixture. 5. Coat with a light brushing of non-stick cooking spray on all sides. 6. Transfer the cookies to the Air Fryer and bake them at 340°F for roughly 10 minutes, or until a golden-brown color is achieved. 7. Allow to cool for 5 minutes before serving.

Per Serving: Calories 23; Fat 1.3g; Sodium 40mg; Carbs 2g; Fiber 1g; Sugar 1g; Protein 1g

Chocolate Coconut Brownies

Prep time: 7 minutes| Cook time: 15 minutes| Serves: 8

½ cup coconut oil
2 oz. dark chocolate
1 cup sugar
2½ tablespoons water
4 whisked eggs
¼ teaspoon ground cinnamon
½ teaspoon ground anise star

¼ teaspoon coconut extract
½ teaspoon vanilla extract
1 tablespoon honey
½ cup flour
½ cup desiccated coconut
sugar, to dust

1. Install the wire rack on Level 3. Select the "BAKE" function of Ninja Foodi Smart XL Pro Air Oven, set temperature to 355°F and time to 15 minutes. Select START/STOP to begin preheating. Melt the chocolate and coconut oil in the microwave. 2. Combine the sugar, water, eggs, cinnamon, anise, coconut extract, vanilla, and honey in a large bowl. 3. Stir in the flour and desiccated coconut. Incorporate everything well. 4. Lightly grease a baking dish with butter. Transfer the mixture to the dish. 5. Place the dish in the Air Fryer and bake at 355°F for 15 minutes. 6. Remove from the fryer and allow to cool slightly. 7. Take care when taking it out of the baking dish. Slice it into squares. 8.Dust with sugar before serving.
Per Serving: Calories 80; Fat 6g; Sodium 444mg; Carbs 6g; Fiber 1g; Sugar 4g; Protein 1g

Banana & Vanilla Puffs

Prep time: 7 minutes| Cook time: 8 minutes| Serves: 8

1 package [8-oz.] crescent dinner rolls, refrigerated
1 cup milk
4 oz. instant vanilla pudding

4 oz. cream cheese, softened
2 bananas, peeled and sliced
1 egg, lightly beaten

1. Install the wire rack on Level 3. Select the "BAKE" function of Ninja Foodi Smart XL Pro Air Oven, set temperature to 355°F and time to 10 minutes. Select START/STOP to begin preheating. Roll out the crescent dinner rolls and slice each one into 8 squares. 2. Mix together the milk, pudding, and cream cheese using a whisk. 3. Scoop equal amounts of the mixture into the pastry squares. Add the banana slices on top. 4. Fold the squares around the filling, pressing down on the edges to seal them. 5. Apply a light brushing of the egg to each pastry puff before placing them in the Air Fryer. 6. Bake for 10 minutes.
Per Serving: Calories 104; Fat 2.5g; Sodium 29mg; Carbs 18g; Fiber 4g; Sugar 2g; Protein 3g

Delicious Chocolate Cake

Prep time: 20 minutes| Cook time: 45 minutes| Serves: 8

½ cup sugar
1¼ cups flour
1 teaspoon baking powder
⅓ cup cocoa powder
¼ teaspoon ground cloves
1/8 teaspoon freshly grated nutmeg
Pinch of table salt

1 egg
¼ cup soda of your choice
¼ cup milk
½ stick butter, melted
2 oz. bittersweet chocolate, melted
½ cup hot water

1. Install the wire rack on Level 3. Select the "BAKE" function of Ninja Foodi Smart XL Pro Air Oven, set temperature to 320°F and time to 35 minutes. Select START/STOP to begin preheating. In a bowl, thoroughly combine the dry ingredients. 2. In another bowl, mix together the egg, soda, milk, butter, and chocolate. 3. Combine the two mixtures. Add in the water and stir well. 4. Take a cake pan that can fit inside your Air Fryer and transfer the mixture to the pan. 5. Place a sheet of foil on top and bake for 35 minutes. 6. Remove the foil and bake for further 10 minutes. 7. Frost the cake with buttercream if desired before serving.
Per Serving: Calories 42; Fat 2.8g; Sodium 126mg; Carbs 4g; Fiber 1g; Sugar 1g; Protein 1g

Healthy Banana Oatmeal Cookies

Prep time: 10 minutes| Cook time: 10 minutes| Serves: 6

2 cups quick oats
¼ cup milk

4 ripe bananas, mashed
¼ cup coconut, shredded

1. Install the wire rack on Level 3. Select the "BAKE" function of Ninja Foodi Smart XL Pro Air Oven, set temperature to 350°F and time to 15 minutes. Select START/STOP to begin preheating. 2.Combine all of the ingredients in a bowl. 3. Scoop equal amounts of the cookie dough onto a baking sheet and put it in the Air Fryer. 4. Bake the cookies for 15 minutes.
Per Serving: Calories 1; Fat 0g; Sodium 114mg; Carbs 0g; Fiber 0g; Sugar 0g; Protein 0g

Coconut Currant Pudding

Prep time: 5 minutes. | Cooking time: 20 minutes. | Servings: 6

1 cup red currants, blended
1 cup black currants, blended

3 tablespoons stevia
1 cup coconut cream

1. In a suitable bowl, mix all the recipe ingredients and stir well. Divide into ramekins, put them in the fryer and Cook on "Bake" mode, select level 3, and set its temperature to 340 degrees F /170 degrees C for 20 minutes. Serve the pudding cold.
Per Serving: Calories 551; Fat 29.3 g; Sodium 74 mg; Carbs 73.9g; Fiber 3.5g; Sugar 55.9g; Protein 5g

Sage Red Currants

Prep time: 5 minutes. | Cooking time: 30 minutes. | Servings: 4

7 cups red currants
1 cup swerve

1 cup water
6 sage leaves

1. In a suitable pan that fits your air fryer, mix all the recipe ingredients, toss, put the pan in level 3 of the fryer and Cook on "Air Fry" Mode, select level 3, and set its temperature to 330 degrees F/165 degrees C for 30 minutes. Discard sage leaves, divide into cups and serve cold.
Per Serving: Calories 148; Fat 0.3 g; Sodium 3 mg; Carbs 38.9g; Fiber 0.5g; Sugar 33.9g; Protein 0.6g

Mixed Berry Pastry

Prep time: 10 minutes| Cook time: 15 minutes| Serves: 3

3 pastry dough sheets
½ cup mixed berries, mashed
1 tablespoon honey

2 tablespoons cream cheese
3 tablespoons chopped walnuts
¼ teaspoon vanilla extract

1. Install the wire rack on Level 3. Select the "BAKE" function of Ninja Foodi Smart XL Pro Air Oven, set temperature to 375°F and time to 15 minutes. Select START/STOP to begin preheating. 2. Roll out the pastry sheets and spread the cream cheese over each one. 3. In a bowl, combine the berries, vanilla extract and honey. 4. Cover a baking sheet with parchment paper. 5. Spoon equal amounts of the berry mixture into the center of each sheet of pastry. Scatter the chopped walnuts on top. 6. Fold up the pastry around the filling and press down the edges with the back of a fork to seal them. 7. Transfer the baking sheet to the Air Fryer and cook for approximately 15 minutes.
Per Serving: Calories 716; Fat 62.6g; Sodium 302mg; Carbs 18g; Fiber 8g; Sugar 2g; Protein 34g

Pear & Apple Crisp with Walnuts

Prep time: 10 minutes| Cook time: 20 minutes| Serves: 6

½ lb. apples, cored and chopped
½ lb. pears, cored and chopped
1 cup flour
1 cup sugar
1 tablespoon butter

1 teaspoon ground cinnamon
¼ teaspoon ground cloves
1 teaspoon vanilla extract
¼ cup chopped walnuts
Whipped cream, to serve

1. Install the wire rack on Level 3. Select the "BAKE" function of Ninja Foodi Smart XL Pro Air Oven, set temperature to 340°F and time to 20 minutes. Select START/STOP to begin preheating. Lightly grease a baking dish and place the apples and pears inside. 2. Combine the rest of the ingredients, minus the walnuts and the whipped cream, until a coarse, crumbly texture is achieved. 3. Pour the mixture over the fruits and spread it evenly. Top with the chopped walnuts. 4. Bake for 20 minutes or until the top turns golden brown. 5. When cooked through, serve at room temperature with whipped cream.
Per Serving: Calories 134; Fat 2.8g; Sodium 64mg; Carbs 26g; Fiber 4g; Sugar 8g; Protein 3g

Sweet Breaded Bananas

Prep time: 10 minutes| Cook time: 10 minutes| Serves: 4

4 ripe bananas, peeled and halved
1 tablespoon meal
1 tablespoon cashew, crushed
1 egg, beaten

1 ½ tablespoon coconut oil
¼ cup flour
1½ tablespoons sugar
½ cup friendly bread crumbs

1. Select the "AIR FRY" function of Ninja Foodi Smart XL Pro Air Oven, set temperature to 350°F and time to 10 minutes. Select START/STOP to begin preheating. In a saucepan, heat the coconut oil, toast in the bread crumbs and cook, stirring continuously, for 4 minutes. 2. Transfer the bread crumbs to a bowl. 3. Add in the meal and crushed cashew. Mix well. 4. Coat each of the banana halves in the corn flour, before dipping it in the beaten egg and lastly coating it with the bread crumbs. 5. Put the coated banana halves in the Air Fryer basket. Season with the sugar. Slide basket into rails of Level 3. 6. Air fry for 10 minutes.
Per Serving: Calories 153; Fat 2.8g; Sodium 28mg; Carbs 26g; Fiber 1g; Sugar 1g; Protein 6g

Sweet Butter Fritters

Prep time: 15 minutes| Cook time: 15 minutes| Serves: 16

For the Dough:
4 cups flour
1 teaspoon kosher salt
1 teaspoon sugar
For the Cakes:
1 cup sugar
Pinch of cardamom

3 tablespoons butter, at room temperature
1 packet instant yeast
1 ¼ cups lukewarm water

1 teaspoon cinnamon powder
1 stick butter, melted

1. Select Level 3. Select the "AIR FRY" function of Ninja Foodi Smart XL Pro Air Oven, set temperature to 360°F and time to 10 minutes. Select START/STOP to begin preheating. Place all ingredients in a bowl and combine well. 2. Add in the lukewarm water and mix until a soft, elastic dough forms. 3. Place the dough on a lightly floured surface and lay a greased sheet of aluminum foil on top of the dough. Refrigerate for 5 to 10 minutes. 4. Remove it from the refrigerator and divide it in two. Mold each half into a log and slice it into 20 pieces. 5. In a shallow bowl, combine the sugar, cardamom and cinnamon. 6. Coat the slices with a light brushing of melted butter and the sugar. 7. Spritz Air Fryer basket with cooking spray. 8. Transfer the slices to the fryer and air fry for roughly 10 minutes. Turn each slice once during the baking time. 9. Dust each slice with the sugar before serving.
Per Serving: Calories 134; Fat 2.8g; Sodium 64mg; Carbs 26g; Fiber 4g; Sugar 8g; Protein 3g

Banana & Coconut Cake

Prep time: 15 minutes| Cook time: 60 minutes| Serves: 5

2/3 cup sugar, shaved
2/3 cup unsalted butter
3 eggs
1¼ cups flour
Topping:
sugar to taste, shaved
Walnuts to taste, roughly chopped

1 ripe banana, mashed
½ teaspoon vanilla extract
1/8 teaspoon baking soda
Sea salt to taste

Bananas to taste, sliced

1. Install the wire rack on Level 3. Select the "BAKE" function of Ninja Foodi Smart XL Pro Air Oven, set temperature to 360°F and time to 48 minutes. Select START/STOP to begin preheating. 2. Mix together the flour, baking soda, and a pinch of sea salt. 3. In a separate bowl, combine the butter, vanilla extract and sugar using an electric mixer or a blender, to achieve a fluffy consistency. 4. Beat in the eggs one at a time. 5. Throw in half of the flour mixture and stir thoroughly. Add in the mashed banana and continue to mix. Lastly, throw in the remaining half of the flour mixture and combine until a smooth batter is formed. 6. Transfer the batter to a baking tray and top with the banana slices. 7. Scatter the chopped walnuts on top before dusting with the sugar. 8. Place a sheet of foil over the tray and pierce several holes in it. 9. Put the covered tray in the Air Fryer. Cook for 48 minutes. 10. Decrease the temperature to 320°F, take off the foil, and allow to cook for an additional 10 minutes until golden brown.
Per Serving: Calories 193; Fat 8.9g; Sodium 93mg; Carbs 2g; Fiber 1g; Sugar 0g; Protein 25g

Crunchy Shortbread Cookies

Prep time: 10 minutes| Cook time: 12 minutes| Serves: 10

1½ cups butter
1 cup flour

¾ cup sugar
Cooking spray

1. Install the wire rack on Level 3. Select the "BAKE" function of Ninja Foodi Smart XL Pro Air Oven, set temperature to 350°F and time to 12 minutes. Select START/STOP to begin preheating. 2. In a bowl. combine the flour and sugar. 3. Cut each stick of butter into small chunks. Add the chunks into the flour and the sugar. 4. Blend the butter into the mixture to combine everything well. 5. Use your hands to knead the mixture, forming a smooth consistency. 6. Shape the mixture into 10 equal-sized finger shapes, marking them with the tines of a fork for decoration if desired. 7. Lightly spritz the Air Fryer basket with the cooking spray. Place the cookies inside, spacing them out well. 8. Bake the cookies for 12 minutes. Let cool slightly before serving. Alternatively, you can store the cookies in an airtight container for up to 3 days.
Per Serving: Calories 292; Fat 24.3g; Sodium 660mg; Carbs 5g; Fiber 0g; Sugar 3g; Protein 14g

Roasted Cinnamon Pumpkin Seeds

Prep time: 15 minutes| Cook time: 20 minutes| Serves: 2

1 cup pumpkin raw seeds
1 tablespoon ground cinnamon
2 tablespoons sugar

1 cup water
1 tablespoon olive oil

1. In a frying pan, combine the pumpkin seeds, cinnamon and water. 2. Boil the mixture over a high heat for 2 - 3 minutes. 3. Pour out the water and place the seeds on a clean kitchen towel, allowing them to dry for 20 - 30 minutes. 4. In a bowl, mix together the sugar, dried seeds, a pinch of cinnamon and one tablespoon of olive oil. 5. Install the wire rack on Level 3. Select the "AIR ROAST" function of Ninja Foodi Smart XL Pro Air Oven, set temperature to 340°F and time to 15 minutes. Select START/STOP to begin preheating. 6.Place the seed mixture in the fryer basket and allow to cook for 15 minutes, shaking the basket periodically throughout.
Per Serving: Calories 101; Fat 5.4g; Sodium 106mg; Carbs 8g; Fiber 3g; Sugar 3g; Protein 7g

Pineapple & Coconut Sticks

Prep time: 10 minutes| Cook time: 10 minutes| Serves: 4

½ fresh pineapple, cut into sticks

¼ cup desiccated coconut

1. Select Level 3. Select the "AIR FTY" function of Ninja Foodi Smart XL Pro Air Oven, set temperature to 400°F and time to 10 minutes. Select START/STOP to begin preheating. 2. Coat the pineapple sticks in the desiccated coconut and put each one in the Air Fryer basket. Air fry for 10 minutes.

Per Serving: Calories 147; Fat 7.3g; Sodium 56mg; Carbs 20g; Fiber 5g; Sugar 11g; Protein 4g

Double Lemon Cake

Prep time: 15 minutes| Cook time: 35 minutes| Serves: 8

For the Cake:
9 oz. sugar
9 oz. butter
3 eggs
9 oz. flour

1 teaspoon vanilla extract
Zest of 1 lemon
1 teaspoon baking powder

For the Frosting:
Juice of 1 lemon
Zest of 1 lemon
1 teaspoon yellow food coloring

7 oz. sugar
4 egg whites

1. Install the wire rack on Level 3. Select the "BAKE" function of Ninja Foodi Smart XL Pro Air Oven, set temperature to 320°F and time to 15 minutes. Select START/STOP to begin preheating.2.Use an electric mixer to combine all of the cake ingredients. 3.Grease the insides of two round cake pans. 4.Pour an equal amount of the batter into each pan. 5.Place one pan in the fryer and cook for 15 minutes, before repeating with the second pan. 6. Mix all of the frosting ingredients.7. Allow the cakes to cool. Spread the frosting and stack the other cake on top.

Per Serving: Calories 162; Fat 9.4g; Sodium 68mg; Carbs 21g; Fiber 4g; Sugar 16g; Protein 1g

Tasty Apple Turnovers

Prep time: 5 minutes| Cook time: 30 minutes| Serves: 4

3½ ounces (100 g) dried apples (about 2½ cups)
¼ cup (35 g) golden raisins
1 tablespoon (13 g) granulated sugar
1 tablespoon (15 ml) freshly squeezed lemon juice
½ teaspoon cinnamon

1 pound (455 g) frozen puff pastry, defrosted according to package instructions
1 egg beaten with 1 tablespoon (15 ml) water
Turbinado or demerara sugar for sprinkling

1. Install the wire rack on Level 3. Select the "BAKE" function of Ninja Foodi Smart XL Pro Air Oven, set temperature to 325°F and time to 30 minutes. Select START/STOP to begin preheating. Place the dried apples in a medium saucepan and cover with about 2 cups (480 ml) of water. Bring the mixture to a boil over medium-high heat, then reduce the heat to low, cover, and simmer until the apples have absorbed most of the liquid, about 20 minutes. Remove the apples from the heat and allow to cool. Add the raisins, sugar, lemon juice, and cinnamon to the rehydrated apples and set aside. 2. On a well-floured board, roll the puff pastry out to a 12-inch (30 cm) square. Cut the square into 4 equal quarters. Divide the filling equally among the 4 squares, mounding it in the middle of each square. Brush the edges of each square with water and fold the pastry diagonally over the apple mixture, creating a triangle. Seal the edges by pressing them with the tines of a fork. Transfer the turnovers to a sheet pan lined with parchment paper. 3. Brush the top of 2 turnovers with egg wash and sprinkle with turbinado sugar. Make 2 small slits in the top of the turnovers for venting and bake for 25 to 30 minutes, until the top is browned and puffed and the pastry is cooked through. Remove the cooked turnovers to a cooling rack and cook the remaining 2 turnovers in the same manner. Serve warm or at room temperature.

Per Serving: Calories 354; Fat 7.9g; Sodium 704mg; Carbs 6g; Fiber 3.6g; Sugar 6g; Protein 18g

Delicious Chocolate Lava Cake

Prep time: 10 minutes| Cook time: 12 minutes| Serves: 4

1 cup dark cocoa candy melts
1 stick butter
2 eggs
4 tablespoons sugar
1 tablespoon honey

4 tablespoons flour
Pinch of kosher salt
Pinch of ground cloves
¼ teaspoon grated nutmeg
¼ teaspoon cinnamon powder

1. Install the wire rack on Level 3. Select the "BAKE" function of Ninja Foodi Smart XL Pro Air Oven, set temperature to 350°F and time to 12 minutes. Select START/STOP to begin preheating. Spritz the insides of four custard cups with cooking spray. 2. Melt the cocoa candy melts and butter in the microwave for 30 seconds to 1 minute. 3. In a large bowl, combine the eggs, sugar and honey with a whisk until frothy. Pour in the melted chocolate mix. 4. Throw in the rest of the ingredients and combine well with an electric mixer or a manual whisk. 5. Transfer equal portions of the mixture into the prepared custard cups. 6. Place in the Air Fryer and air bake for 12 minutes. 7. Cool for 5 to 6 minutes. 8. Place each cup upside-down on a dessert plate and let the cake slide out. Serve with fruits and chocolate syrup if desired.
Per Serving: Calories 88; Fat 7.1g; Sodium 143mg; Carbs 4g; Fiber 3g; Sugar 1g; Protein 4g

Homemade Blueberry Pancakes

Prep time: 10 minutes| Cook time: 10 minutes| Serves: 4

½ teaspoon vanilla extract
2 tablespoons honey
½ cup blueberries
½ cup sugar
2 cups + 2 tablespoon flour

3 eggs, beaten
1 cup milk
1 teaspoon baking powder
Pinch of salt

1. Install the wire rack on Level 3. Select the "BAKE" function of Ninja Foodi Smart XL Pro Air Oven, set temperature to 390°F and time to 10 minutes. Select START/STOP to begin preheating. 2. In a bowl, mix together all of the dry ingredients. 3. Pour in the wet ingredients and combine with a whisk, ensuring the mixture becomes smooth. 4. Roll each blueberry in some flour to lightly coat it before folding it into the mixture. This is to ensure they do not change the color of the batter. 5. Coat the inside of a baking dish with a little oil or butter. 6. Spoon several equal amounts of the batter onto the baking dish, spreading them into pancake shapes and ensuring to space them out well. This may have to be completed in two batches. 7. Place the dish in the fryer and bake for about 10 minutes.
Per Serving: Calories 139; Fat 3.2g; Sodium 45mg; Carbs 26g; Fiber 4g; Sugar 8g; Protein 3g

Lemon Tarts

Prep time: 15 minutes| Cook time: 15 minutes| Serves: 4

½ cup butter
½ lb. flour
2 tablespoons sugar

1 large lemon, juiced and zested
2 tablespoons lemon curd
Pinch of nutmeg

1. In a large bowl, combine the butter, flour and sugar until a crumbly consistency is achieved. 2. Add in the lemon zest and juice, followed by a pinch of nutmeg. Continue to combine. 3. Sprinkle the insides of a few small pastry tins with flour. Pour equal portions of the dough into each one and add sugar or lemon zest on top. 4. Select Level 3. Select the "AIR FRY" function of Ninja Foodi Smart XL Pro Air Oven, set temperature to 360°F and time to 15 minutes. Select START/STOP to begin preheating. 5. Place the lemon tarts inside the fryer and allow to cook for 15 minutes.
Per Serving: Calories 4; Fat 0.1g; Sodium 0mg; Carbs 1g; Fiber 1g; Sugar 0g; Protein 0g

Pumpkin Cake

Prep time: 15 minutes| Cook time: 35 minutes| Serves: 4

1 large egg
½ cup skimmed milk
7 oz. flour
2 tablespoons sugar

5 oz. pumpkin puree
Pinch of salt
Pinch of cinnamon [if desired]
Cooking spray

1. Stir together the pumpkin puree and sugar in a bowl. Crack in the egg and combine using a whisk until smooth. 2. Add in the flour and salt, stirring constantly. Pour in the milk, ensuring to combine everything well. 3. Spritz a baking tin with cooking spray. 4. Transfer the batter to the baking tin. 5. Install the wire rack on Level 3. Select the "BAKE" function of Ninja Foodi Smart XL Pro Air Oven, set temperature to 350°F and time to 15 minutes. Select START/STOP to begin preheating. 6. Put the tin in the Air Fryer basket and bake for 15 minutes.

Per Serving: Calories 409; Fat 18.9g; Sodium 214mg; Carbs 10g; Fiber 1g; Sugar 9g; Protein 48g

Crispy Apple Wedges

Prep time: 10 minutes| Cook time: 15 minutes| Serves: 4

4 large apples
2 tablespoons olive oil
½ cup dried apricots, chopped

1-2 tablespoons sugar
½ teaspoon ground cinnamon

1. Select Level 3. Select the "AIR FRY" function of Ninja Foodi Smart XL Pro Air Oven, set temperature to 350°F and time to 12 minutes. Select START/STOP to begin preheating. Peel the apples and slice them into eight wedges. Throw away the cores. 2. Coat the apple wedges with the oil. 3.Place each wedge in the Air Fryer and cook for 12 - 15 minutes. 4. Add in the apricots and allow to cook for a further 3 minutes. 5. Stir together the sugar and cinnamon. Sprinkle this mixture over the cooked apples before serving.

Per Serving: Calories 271; Fat 9.3g; Sodium 15mg; Carbs 43g; Fiber 6g; Sugar 2g; Protein 5g

Cherry Turnovers

Prep time: 10 minutes. | Cooking time: 56 minutes. | Servings: 8

2 sheets frozen puff pastry, thawed
1 (21-ounce) can premium cherry pie filling
2 teaspoons ground cinnamon
1 egg, beaten

1 cup sliced almonds
1 cup powdered sugar
2 tablespoons milk

1. Spread a sheet of puff pastry out into a square that is approximately 10-inches by 10-inches. Cut this large square into quarters. 2. Mix the cherry pie filling and cinnamon in a suitable bowl. Spoon ¼ cup of the cherry filling into the center of each puff pastry square. Brush the perimeter of the pastry square with the egg wash. Fold one corner of the puff pastry over the cherry pie filling towards the opposite corner, forming a triangle. Seal the two edges of the pastry with the tip of a fork, making a design with the tines. Brush the egg wash on the top of the turnovers and sprinkle sliced almonds over each one. Repeat these steps with the second sheet of puff pastry. You should have eight turnovers at the end. 3. Select Air Fry mode, pre-heat the air fryer to 370 degrees F/ 185 degrees C. Select Level "3" and set the time on your Ninja Foodi Smart XL Pro Air Fryer Oven to 14 minutes. Press Start/Pause to begin preheating. Continue to the next step when it is done preheating. 4. Insert the basket in the level 3 of the Ninja Foodi Smart XL Pro Oven. 5. Air-fry two turnovers at a time for 14 minutes, carefully turning them over halfway through the Cooking time. 6. While the turnovers are cooking, make the glaze by whisking the powdered sugar and milk in a suitable bowl until smooth. Let the glaze sit for a minute. 7. Let the cooked cherry turnovers sit for at least 10 minutes. Then drizzle the glaze over each turnover in a zigzag motion. Serve warm or at room temperature.

Per Serving: Calories 506; Fat 48.3 g; Sodium 608 mg; Carbs 158.9g; Fiber 6.5g; Sugar 83.9g; Protein 12.6g

Conclusion

With its revolutionary appearance and extensive functionality, the Ninja Foodi XL Pro Air Oven DT250 is the most user-friendly of all the toaster ovens we examined. If you're searching for an oven that can serve you at every meal, despite taking up quite a bit of countertop space in your kitchen (17 x 20 x 13 inches), this one is definitely worth the investment. It performs every task flawlessly, including toasting bread, reheating frozen pizza, baking, and roasting. Additionally, it has the ability to air fry, giving you the capability of multiple appliances in a single unit.

Yes, if you're looking for a countertop convection oven with a variety of cooking options, I'd highly recommend the Ninja Foodi Smart XL Pro Air Oven. It's superior to a full-sized convection oven, in my opinion.

Appendix 1 Measurement Conversion Chart

VOLUME EQUIVALENTS (LIQUID)

US STANDARD	US STANDARD (OUNCES)	METRIC (APPROXIMATE)
2 tablespoons	1 fl.oz	30 mL
¼ cup	2 fl.oz	60 mL
½ cup	4 fl.oz	120 mL
1 cup	8 fl.oz	240 mL
1½ cup	12 fl.oz	355 mL
2 cups or 1 pint	16 fl.oz	475 mL
4 cups or 1 quart	32 fl.oz	1 L
1 gallon	128 fl.oz	4 L

VOLUME EQUIVALENTS (DRY)

US STANDARD	METRIC (APPROXIMATE)
⅛ teaspoon	0.5 mL
¼ teaspoon	1 mL
½ teaspoon	2 mL
¾ teaspoon	4 mL
1 teaspoon	5 mL
1 tablespoon	15 mL
¼ cup	59 mL
½ cup	118 mL
¾ cup	177 mL
1 cup	235 mL
2 cups	475 mL
3 cups	700 mL
4 cups	1 L

TEMPERATURES EQUIVALENTS

FAHRENHEIT(F)	CELSIUS(C) (APPROXIMATE)
225 °F	107 °C
250 °F	120 °C
275 °F	135 °C
300 °F	150 °C
325 °F	160 °C
350 °F	180 °C
375 °F	190 °C
400 °F	205 °C
425 °F	220 °C
450 °F	235 °C
475 °F	245 °C
500 °F	260 °C

WEIGHT EQUIVALENTS

US STANDARD	METRIC (APPROXINATE)
1 ounce	28 g
2 ounces	57 g
5 ounces	142 g
10 ounces	284 g
15 ounces	425 g
16 ounces (1 pound)	455 g
1.5pounds	680 g
2pounds	907 g

Appendix 2 Air Fryer Cooking Chart

Vegetables	Temp	Time (min)
Asparagus	375°F	4 to 6
Baked Potatoes	400°F	35 to 45
Broccoli	400°F	8 to 10
Brussels Sprouts	350°F	15 to 18
Butternut Squash (cubed)	375°F	20 to 25
Carrots	375°F	15 to 25
Cauliflower	400°F	10 to 12
Corn on the Cob	390°F	6
Eggplant	400°F	15
Green Beans	375°F	16 to 20
Kale	250°F	12
Mushrooms	400°F	5
Peppers	375°F	8 to 10
Sweet Potatoes (whole)	380°F	30 to 35
Tomatoes (halved, sliced)	350°F	10
Zucchini (½-inch sticks)	400°F	12

Desserts	Temp	Time (min)
Apple Pie	320°F	30
Brownies	350°F	17
Churros	360°F	13
Cookies	350°F	5
Cupcakes	330°F	11
Doughnuts	360°F	5
Roasted Bananas	375°F	8
Peaches	350°F	5

Meat and Seafood	Temp	Time (min)
Bacon	400°F	5 to 10
Beef Eye Round Roast (4 lbs)	390°F	45 to 55
Bone to in Pork Chops	400°F	4 to 5 per side
Brats	400°F	8 to 10
Burgers	350°F	8 to 10
Chicken Breast	375°F	22 to 23
Chicken Tender	400°F	14 to 16
Chicken Thigh	400°F	25
Chicken Wings (2 lbs)	400°F	10 to 12
Cod	370°F	8 to 10
Fillet Mignon (8oz)	400°F	14 to 18
Fish Fillet (0.5 lb., 1-inch)	400°F	10
Flank Steak(1.5 lbs)	400°F	10 to 14
Lobster Tails (4oz)	380°F	5 to 7
Meatballs	400°F	7 to 10
Meat Loaf	325°F	35 to 45
Pork Chops	375°F	12 to 15
Salmon	400°F	5 to 7
Salmon Fillet (6oz)	380°F	12
Sausage Patties	400°F	8 to 10
Shrimp	375°F	8
Steak	400°F	7 to 14
Tilapia	400°F	8 to 12
Turkey Breast (3 lbs)	360°F	40 to 50
Whole Chicken (6.5 lbs)	360°F	75

Frozen Foods	Temp	Time (min)
Breaded Shrimp	400°F	9
Chicken Burger	360°F	11
Chicken Nudgets	400°F	10
Corn Dogs	400°F	7
Curly Fries (1 to 2 lbs)	400°F	11 to 14
Fish Sticks (10oz)	400°F	10
French Fries	380°F	15 to 20
Hash Brown	360°F	15 to 18
Meatballs	380°F	6 to 8
Mozzarella Sticks	400°F	8
Onion Rings (8oz)	400°F	8
Pizza	390°F	5 to 10
Pot Pie	360°F	25
Pot Sticks (10oz)	400°F	8
Sausage Rolls	400°F	15
Spring Rolls	400°F	15 to 20

Appendix 3 Recipes Index

Made in the USA
Las Vegas, NV
08 July 2024